MW01485725

Buying My First Home As A Military Veteran

A Veteran's Homebuying Guide

By

Brian K. Bailey

To MY BESTIE!

Thanks For your Many years
OF Support!

Thanks For your Service!

Thanks For being an
Amazing FRIEND!

Love Ya,

i

Buying My First Home as a Military Veteran
A Veteran's Homebuying Guide

© 2017 Home Tyme Publishing

All rights reserved. No portion of this book may be reproduced, stored in a retrieval system, or transmitted in any form or by any means – electronic, mechanical, photocopy, recording, scanning or other, except for brief quotations in critical reviews or articles, without the prior written permission of the publisher.

Published in Atlanta, Georgia by Home Tyme Publishing

Cover design by James E. Roach II

To order additional copies of this book or the audio book contact:

Brian K. Bailey
www.militarybuyhomes.com

In an effort to support our local veteran communities, raise awareness and funds, Brian K. Bailey donates a percentage of all book sales to VAREP Cares through the organization named Veterans Association of Real Estate Professionals. VAREP Cares supports active military and veterans as a result of hardship. Every person that has honorably served, deserve assistance when they need a hand up. VAREP Cares is that place. For more information about this program visit www.varep.net.

MESSAGE FROM THE AUTHOR

As a retired military member, buying my home using the VA loan was one of my greatest accomplishments. I have been able to enjoy the benefits of homeownership for over 20 years. When I started the home buying process in 1997, I didn't have the knowledge that I have today. Twenty years ago, there were not as many resources for veterans who wanted to buy a home. You had to do your own research and pray that it all worked out. Today, you have more information at your disposal. There are many organizations that are willing to help, but buying a home as a military veteran is still an educational process.

As I spoke to industry professionals and interviewed military members, I've learned there are many qualified military veterans who have not purchased a home and what's more surprising was the amount of veterans who have not used their VA Loan benefit.

According to a MarketWatch 2014 survey, only 36 percent of Iraq and Afghanistan Veterans of America (IAVA) indicated they had sought a VA loan. In its Veteran's Affairs Blog, the VA affirms that misconceptions and a lack of information have kept millions of potential VA loan aspirants from exploring their options.

A common misconception among vets, the VA Blog added, was that the application process is cumbersome and takes too long for approval. However, 70 percent of VA loans in 2014 had closed in 90 days or less, compared with 61 percent of FHA applications and 67 percent of conventional home loans.

You owe it to yourself to find out what the VA home loan program has to offer. In my opinion as a veteran homeowner, I believe buying your first home as a military veteran will be one of your greatest victories.

Together, we can complete this mission!

"Every military veteran deserves to be a Veteran Homeowner"

Brian K. Bailey

****

FREE GIFT

I wanted to give you access to a special gift for buying this book.

VA Homebuying
Frequently Asked Questions (FAQs)

Claim your FREE GIFT @

Bonus.TheVeteranHomeOwner.com

****

DEDICATION

This book is dedicated to all of the military veterans who proudly serve and have served our country. As a fellow veteran, I say, "Thank you!" Thank you for your selfless service. Thank you for facing grave dangers in order to keep America safe. Thank you to those who came before me and those who have fallen.

I Salute You!

ACKNOWLEDGEMENT AND SUPPORT

I would like to take time to acknowledge some special people who were a part of this book!

- Artri Spratling
- Sonya McCall
- Kim Williams
- Ellissa Mitchell
- Beatrice Jones
- Juernene "Chippy" Bass
- and... Taurea Vision Avant (My book writing coach) *www.showyoursuccess.com*

I also have to thank these industry professionals who have helped me with the knowledge and the education needed in order to provide this much needed content to our veterans

- Jim and Tina Hyatt – Exit Results Realty
- LeeAnne Rodriques – Pride Settlement and Escrow, LLC
- Markita Woods also known as "The Queen of Mortgages" *www.queenofmortgages.com* NMLS #196099
- Margo S. Morgan-Valentin – Morgan Realty and Management Services Inc.
- Glenford Blanc – Pro-Spex Professional Home Inspection Service

- Chris Bridges – Credit with Chris
  www.goodcreditwithchris.com
- Christine Olfus – DC Chapter President
  *Veteran Association of Real Estate Professionals
  (VAREP)
- Lewis C. Hibbs Jr. – Renovation Sales Manager
  AnnieMac Home Mortgage NMLS #270092

*A special acknowledgement is in order for **VAREP**. As my way of giving back to my military brothers and sisters, I am donating 5% of every book sale to a VAREP program called VAREP Cares. VAREP Cares supports active military and veterans as a result of hardship. Every person that has honorably served, deserve assistance when they need a hand up. VAREP Cares is that place. For more information about this program visit www.varep.net.

The final thanks go out to my family who has always supported my vision and mission when it comes to helping others.

May this book be a blessing not only to all who reads it but also to those who took the time to support this project. I appreciate each and everyone one of you!

TESTIMONIALS

Legal Disclaimer: Individual Results May Vary

Veteran Homeowners are my motivation behind this book. Their stories prove that homeownership is truly the American dream. The VA loan process not only helped me purchase my first home but it gave me a great feeling of pride and accomplishment. This same feeling is shared by many of my fellow veterans from around the world. ***We are the Veteran Homebuyers of America.***

"I couldn't have lived the American Dream without a VA Loan. As a single woman with good credit, I was able to buy my own house and even got my earnest money back at closing with no other down payment. I was also able to refinance without paying the refinance fees. Sure fees are rolled in, but at least I still have my savings."

Adrienne Saint, U.S. Air Force

"Having the opportunity to serve in the United States Air Force afforded me the privilege to use the VA benefit many service members are unaware they qualify for. I first learned about VA home loans thanks to the awesome realtor I was fortunate to select. As a first-time homebuyer, my realtor provided me with all the financial purchasing options that included the VA loan. The one factor that stood out the most amongst the options was 'no down payment.' Using the VA home loan was such a simple process that I used it again to build a home. 'No down payment' is so attractive, it allows you to keep money in your pocket to purchase the necessities that go along with a new or previously owned home. If you've ever served in the military, find a realtor that can help determine if you are eligible for a VA home loan and reap one of the many benefits of having served our great country."

Karen J. Clay U.S. Air Force, Retired

"In 2002, after getting a divorce I used my VA certificate to purchase a new townhome. My first choice was to rent an apartment but because I didn't have the first month rent and security deposit, rent wasn't an option. Using the VA certificate allowed me to get approved for a loan from the bank with an offer for a new job and with no money down."

Phyliss King U.S. Army Retired

"I am one of more than 21 million veterans that the Department of Veterans Affairs has assisted in buying a home. I used the VA home loan program in buying four homes; I sold three and one I still own. This program has helped me greatly in purchasing a home at my various duty stations where on post housing was not available, adequate for my family or renting a home didn't make sense. It made financial sense to me especially when money was tight during my early Army career. I have enjoyed the VA Home Loan Program benefits of no down payment, no mortgage insurance, low interest rate, almost no closing costs, and easy credit check. I do remember that each of the mortgage companies I worked with in purchasing my homes, were very happy working with me. This is due to how easy the contract was and how fast the closing process went. I will be using the VA Home Loan Program again in the near future when I purchase my Army retirement home in Colorado. All you need is a DD214 to get the ball rolling! You would be crazy not to use this exclusive VA benefit. Blessings and Good Luck!"

Douglas Mohr, U.S. Army

"My wife and I thank the VA for giving us a chance to use our VA Loans to buy not just one but two homes. I hope you enjoy the purchase of your home as much as my family is enjoying ours."

Darren Rutherford, U.S. Army

"In 2010, I requested my home loan paperwork. My wife and I were looking for a home to purchase in the Florida Keys. Once we settled on a price, I turned that single piece of paper over to my Realtor and he did all of the work for us. It could not have been any easier! Zero down and lower interest rates to boot."

Robert Jankowski, U.S. Air Force Retired

"My husband and I are so thankful for the VA mortgage loan program. Military life with all its moves can make creating a 'home' difficult. Because the VA offers zero down we could buy our own home, not once but three times. We have enjoyed this benefit even after retirement. Having a guide to walk us through the steps has been invaluable."

Christi M. Rendon, Air Force Spouse

"I brought my first home, a brand new 3 bedroom, 2 ½ bath using my VA Loan. I was able to put zero money down which allowed me to utilize that money in other ways. It was truly a blessing."

Robin A. Proudie, U.S. Navy

CONTENTS

INTRODUCTION

This book is not just about how I achieved mission success when buying my first home as a military veteran. Even though the title is *"Buying My First Home As A Military Veteran"*, the story line quickly goes from learning about how I got started and transitions into helping you complete the process for yourself. I call it a Veteran Homebuyer's "Battle Book", as it will cover everything from going through the credit improvement process, selecting the right lender, real estate agent, finding the right home and making it to settlement a.k.a. the day you get the keys to your new brand new home. I have also included a few bonuses along the way!

A home is what many call the American Dream. I also see buying a home as part of the growing up process. I remember as a young Air Force Technical Sergeant taking my dog Georgio on these long walks when I lived in a rental property in Severn, Maryland. These walks would frequently take us into the area where townhomes and single-family homes lined the streets. I would look at the different styles, colors, configurations and landscapes. Taking these relaxing walks with my four-legged friend began to put me in the mindset of wanting a home to call my own.

As my goal of wanting a home started to grow stronger, I started doing things that aligned my life towards the path of home buying success. You see, when I put my mind to something, there is a good chance that I will make my goal a reality. I remember spending weekends visiting many beautiful new home communities. I did have a price range in mind but that never stopped me from going to visit those big 10,000 square foot mini mansion model homes on Saturday mornings. Visiting multiple homes that would cost upwards of a million dollars was not part of my reality at that time, but it allowed me to dream of what could be. Truth be told, based on my salary as that young Technical Sergeant, I knew I could only afford a certain amount of money per month, and a million dollar home was not in my price range.

When reality really started to kick in, it became apparent that I had to take a good look at my current financial situation. I had to ask myself some important questions such as: How's my credit and is it good enough to buy the type of home that I want to purchase? What is my monthly affordability range? Are there certain types of homes that will fit within my monthly affordability range? What are my benefits as a member of the military? These are some of the questions that ran through my mind as I began to mentally prepare for the process of home ownership.

The next question was: where do I go for answers? At the time, I didn't have anyone to point me in the right direction and I don't think we had a good Internet search engine as Google wasn't created yet. So, I went searching for answers but my list of people to get answers from was not big at the time as most of my military peers lived on base or were renting an apartment just like me. At this point in my military career I was assigned to Andrews AFB. If you wanted to live in On-base housing you had to be married. If you wanted to live off base, you would receive BAH (Base Allowance for Housing) which in my case, based on my rank, would have been around $1800 per month. Along with my base salary, my BAH would give me a good starting point based on what I could afford.

Even though in my mind I was ready to buy a home, my financial foundation was very shaky. I had way too many bills. Not only did I have too many bills but some of my accounts were overdue. Not to mention my spending habits were all over the place. In order to be considered for a loan, I had to get my finances in order quick. So I made up my mind to fix it up. I dug into my financial foxhole and went to work. Again, when I set my mind to something, I find a way to achieve mission success.

Long story short, I have been a homeowner for over 20 years and I will tell anyone, taking advantage of my military benefits when it came to homeownership was the smartest financial decision I've ever made.

Now that I shared a little bit of my homebuying journey with you, let me share something else. I am big on giveaways as you will see when you visit my website titled **bonus.theveteranhomeowner.com**.

Buying My First Home As A Military Veteran will give you a lot of information when it comes to the homebuying process, but I can't fit everything in this book. So in an effort to keep you current on updates, changes, and must have information that is not in the book, I created a website where you can get that extra data. When you go to the website, make sure you register with your name and email address and in return, you will have special access to your very own "homebuying coach."

3

This site will also be a great homebuying resource as you go through the homebuying process. I look forward to meeting you online!

Since we are talking about giveaways, my first giveaway is already included inside of this book and it's called The VA Homebuyer's Journal. The VA Homebuyer's Journal is a special gift that allows you to jot down the names of your home buying "Success Team" along with capturing important information as you go through your home buying journey.

Your home buying "Success Team" will be those professionals who will lead you through your home buying mission. Your team will be made up of (as a minimum) your Real Estate Agent, Lender, and a Title Company Representative. Your VA Homebuyer's Journal is a tool that will assist you greatly during the home buying process.

Let me end this introduction by saying congratulations on taking a big step toward homeownership. It's a memorable journey that should bring many years of enjoyment. If you find this book to be a great resource for you, please share it with other military veterans or send them to **www.militarybuyhomes.com** so they can receive their very own signed copy!

Good luck on your homebuying journey and thanks for your service.

Respectively,

Brian K. Bailey, U.S. Air Force (Retired)

©Glasbergen
glasbergen.com

"It's not bad for our first home. You'll like it better
after I add a fireplace, more closets, and a deck."

Reprinted by permission. Drawing by Randy Glasbergen

CHAPTER 1 – YOUR CREDIT

*"The ache for home lives in all of us. The safe place where
we can go as we are and not be questioned."*

~ Maya Angelou

For my entire military career, I had to focus on staying in shape. But my preparation for fitness excellence couldn't start the day before my fitness test. It involved a year of steady focused effort. When it comes to improving your credit, you should take the same approach. Steady focused effort along with a little preplanning goes a long way, especially if you are planning to purchase a home in the near or distant future.

In this chapter, we are going to discuss how to prep for credit success, so when it's time to purchase your home, you have a strong credit based foundation. The steps that I will cover worked for me and many others and I believe if you follow my suggested steps, they will work for you as well.

If you want to purchase a home you have two options; the first option is to pay cash. Most people aren't in a position financially to do that. So that leaves us with option number two, which is to finance the property or in real estate speak, take out a mortgage. Option two begins with and is based on your current credit standing. I like to consider your credit standing as being the foundation of your home buying process.

In order to know your credit standing, you must begin with having a copy of your credit report. Your credit report speaks to the lender about your financial stability and it also helps them identify your risk factor. What is risk factor you ask? It's how a bank views a person's ability to pay back a loan.

If you have been late on your bills a certain number of times, or you have a high debt to income ratio, your ability to pay your bills may be at jeopardy. You may get a loan but there is a good chance that you will pay a higher interest rate. The opposite applies to the person who pays their bills on time and keeps their debts low. This person will get the lowest interest rate and as a result, will be able to buy more home for the money.

Your credit report contains information about where you live, how you pay your bills, and whether you've been sued or arrested, or have filed for bankruptcy. Credit reporting companies sell the information in your report to creditors, insurers, employers, and other businesses that use it to evaluate your applications for credit, insurance, employment, or buying/renting a home. The federal Fair Credit Reporting Act (FCRA) promotes the accuracy and privacy of information in the files of the nation's credit reporting companies. The information in your credit report is what the lender uses to determine whether or not you are going to get the money you are asking for. If you want to see your credit picture, you must be proactive in obtaining the right information. Fortunately, there are many ways to gain access to your credit status.

How to Order Your Free Report

An amendment to the FCRA requires each of the nationwide credit reporting companies (Equifax, Experian, and TransUnion) to provide you with a FREE copy of your credit report at your request, once every 12 months.

The three nationwide credit reporting companies have set up one website, a toll-free telephone number, and a mailing address through which you can order your free annual report. To order, visit annualcreditreport.com or call 1-877-322-8228 and ask for a copy of the Annual Credit Report Request Form. Once you receive the form, mail it to:

Annual Credit Report Request Service
P.O. Box 105281
Atlanta, GA 30348-5281

I want to give you an idea of how my credit information changed after contacting the three credit reporting companies. Mind you, this was before the Annual Credit Report Request service was available. I had to personally contact each agency individually and ask for my FREE credit report. What I found out didn't surprise me, but it gave me an idea of what I needed to work on. I had some overdue bills and yes, I even had a judgment on my record that had not yet been removed. Initially I thought I needed to have perfect credit to buy a home, but actually all I needed to do was work on some of my credit issues in order to get an approval. My solution at the time (about 20 years ago) was to go to a credit counselor and debt repayment agency. That was a great idea as it allowed me to set up a debt repayment plan.

My credit turn-around was not something that happened in one day; it took about six to nine months to get some of those issues cleared up. But I can tell you this; it was because of my focus and determination that I was able to get this done. This should speak to you right now in regard to when to start looking for a home and it should say, don't look for a home until you have all of your credit ducks in a row. In order to know where you stand in regard to your credit, there are a few steps you can take right away.

Check Your Credit Score

Credit score repair begins with your credit report. I know I mentioned this earlier in this chapter, but make sure you contact the Annual Credit Report Service to get a copy of your credit report from the three reporting agencies. Each agency may have different comments or items that may need to be disputed. So go over each one with a fine-toothed comb. Check to make sure that there are no late payments incorrectly listed for any of your accounts and that the amounts owed for each of your open accounts is correct. Unfortunately, credit errors are not uncommon. According to a 2013 survey conducted by the Federal Trade Commission, 25 percent of credit reports contain errors. Although some of the errors may be minor to include misspelled names or addresses, a large amount were serious enough to result in denial of credit.

If you discover errors, contact the credit reporting agencies and creditors immediately in writing. Explain the errors, provide documentation to back up your claims, and request that the items be removed or adjusted. Check back often to ensure your claim is receiving appropriate attention.

Search and Destroy

As we get into more detail on fixing your credit, I must let you know that in order to get this done you really have to be determined and focused while going through the process. I will tell you there are companies that will charge you hundreds of dollars to assist in your credit restoration and you may choose to go that route, but let me just show you what two steps are recommended via the Federal Trade Commission (FTC) website (*consumer.ftc.gov*).

Under the FCRA, both the credit reporting company and the information provider (that is, the person, company, or organization that provides information about you to a credit reporting company) are responsible for correcting inaccurate or incomplete information in your report. To take advantage of all your rights under this law, contact the credit reporting company and the information provider.

Step One

Tell the credit reporting company in writing what information you think is inaccurate. *The FTC has a **sample dispute letter** for you to use, which can be found via* **Bonus.TheVeteranHomeowner.com**. Include copies (NOT originals) of documents that support your position. In addition to providing your complete name and address, your letter should clearly identify each item in your credit report that you are disputing. State the facts and explain why you are disputing the information and request that it be removed or corrected. You may want to enclose a copy of your credit report with the items in question circled. Send your letter by certified mail, "return receipt requested," so you can document what the credit reporting company received. Keep copies of your dispute letter and enclosures.

Credit reporting companies must investigate the items in question — usually within 30 days unless they consider your dispute frivolous. They also must forward all the relevant data you provide about the inaccuracy to the organization that provided the information. After the information provider receives notice of a dispute from the credit reporting company, it must investigate, review the relevant information, and report the results back to the credit reporting company. If the information provider finds the disputed information is inaccurate, it must notify all three nationwide credit-reporting companies so they can correct the information in your file.

When the investigation is complete, the credit reporting company must give you the results in writing and a free copy of your report if the dispute results in a change. Please note that this free report does not count as your annual free report. If an item is changed or deleted, the credit reporting company cannot put the disputed information back in your file unless the information provider verifies that it is accurate and complete. The credit reporting company also must send you written notice that includes the name, address, and phone number of the information provider.

If you ask, the credit reporting company must send notices of any corrections to anyone who received your report in the past six months. You can also have a corrected copy of your report sent to anyone who received a copy during the past two years for employment purposes.

If an investigation doesn't resolve your dispute with the credit reporting company, you can ask that a statement of the dispute be included in your file and in future reports. You also can ask the credit reporting company to provide your statement to anyone who received a copy of your report in the recent past. You can expect to pay a fee for this service.

Step Two

Tell the information provider (that is, the person, company, or organization that provides information about you to a credit reporting company), in writing, that you are disputing an item in your credit report.

Use the FTC's **sample dispute letter @ Bonus.TheVeteranHomeowner.com**. Make sure you include copies (NOT originals) of documents that support your position. If the provider listed an address on your credit report, send your letter to that address. If no address is listed, contact the provider and ask for the correct address to send your letter. If the information provider does not give you an address, you can send your letter to any business address for that provider.

If the provider continues to report the item you disputed to a credit reporting company, it must let the credit reporting company know about your dispute. If the information you are disputing is found to be inaccurate or incomplete, the information provider must tell the credit reporting company to update or delete the item.

All about your File

Your credit file may not reflect all your credit accounts. Although most national department store and all-purpose bank credit card accounts will be included in your file, not all creditors supply information to credit reporting companies: some local retailers, credit unions, travel, entertainment, and gasoline card companies are among the creditors that don't.

When negative information in your report is accurate, only the passage of time can assure its removal. A credit reporting company can report most accurate negative information for seven years and bankruptcy information for ten years. Information about an unpaid judgment against you can be reported for seven years or until the statute of limitations runs out, whichever is longer. There is no time limit on reporting the following: information about criminal convictions, information reported in response to your application for a job that pays more than $75,000 a year, and information reported because you've applied for more than $150,000 worth of credit or life insurance. There is a standard method for calculating the seven-year reporting period. Generally, the period runs from the date that the event took place.

Setup Payment Reminders

Making your credit payments on time is one of the biggest contributing factors to your credit scores. Some banks offer payment reminders through their online banking portals that can send you an email or text message reminding you when a payment is due. You could also consider enrolling in automatic payments through your credit card and loan providers to have payments automatically debited from your bank account, but this only makes the minimum payment on your credit cards and does not help instill a sense of money management. If you own a phone or a computer, it's also easy enough to set up reminders on your calendar.

Reduce the Amount of Debt You Owe

I know this is easier said than done, but reducing the amount that you owe is going to be a far more of a satisfying achievement than improving your credit score. The first thing you need to do is stop using your credit cards. I mean that, *STOP USING YOUR CREDIT CARDS!* Use your credit report to make a list of all of your accounts and then go online or check recent statements to determine how much you owe on each account and what interest rate they are charging you. Come up with a payment plan that puts most of your available budget for debt payments towards the highest interest cards first, while maintaining minimum payments on your other accounts.

Organize Your Bills

One of the things I was able to do in regard to my bills was keeping track of what I owed and what my payments should be. I learned that I should start with the end in mind. With that said, my goal was to stay focused on getting those bills paid. The hardest part of paying bills is getting organized. When your bills come in, put them all in one area even if it's just in a shoebox. The worst thing you can do is have the first of the month roll around and you can't find your gas and electric bill. I am talking from experience as I used to be the worst when it came to putting my bills in one place. I would just pick up the mail, sort through each piece and throw the stack in a corner. The problem with this is, as we say, "out of sight, out of mind." Can you see why putting your bills in one place makes sense? Let's take it a step further. What if you created a Bills Binder. What I mean is, get yourself a binder from your local office supply store and while you're at it, pick up some file folders. The key is to get enough file folders to match up to all of your bills. In this example, let's start off with your gas and electric bill. If it is due on the 5th of each month, write that down on the folder (Due the 5th of the Month) Repeat this for all your bills. Now you have a system.

As we play catch up with technology we can use applications such as a calendar reminder to tell you when each bill is due or if you want to take it a step further, check to see if your banking institution has what is called "Bill Pay" or something along those lines. I currently use this program with my personal and business accounts. It makes bill paying easier as I can go in and preset the amounts to be paid on my bills. The main thing I want you to understand is the way you pay your bills determines the success you have in the homebuying process. This is foundation stuff and I am really hoping you are getting it.

Credit Building Blocks

I realize not everyone has perfect credit and some may have no credit and all. Whatever category you are in involves going through the building block process. Let's look at those who have okay credit and want to make it better. Here are three success steps for you to follow:

1. Keep your balances low on credit cards and other "revolving credit lines", high outstanding debt can adversely affect your credit score.
2. Pay off your debt rather than moving it around is an effective way to improve your credit scores.
3. Don't open a number of new credit cards that you don't need just to increase your available credit as this approach could backfire and actually lower your credit score.

The question that is asked more by our younger veterans is not how do you fix your credit but more along the lines of how to establish credit. Pay attention to me on this one because even though you may not be in a position to buy a house right now, you are planning to buy in the future. So this is actually a bonus for you.

Building Credit Slowly

Starting off with a secured credit card is a good was to build up your credit. All you are doing is using a secured card that is backed by a cash deposit you make upfront; the deposit amount is usually the same as your credit limit. I can't suggest the best card to use but I do recommend that you do research before you make a selection. You'll use your secured card like any other credit card: buy things, make a payment on or before the due date, incur interest if you don't pay your balance in full. Your cash deposit is used as collateral if you fail to make payments.

Secured credit cards aren't meant to be used forever. The purpose of a secured card is to build your credit enough to qualify for an unsecured card also known as a card without a deposit and with better benefits. Choose a secured card with a low annual fee and make sure it reports to all three credit bureaus, Equifax, Experian and Transunion.

Also note with secured cards you should receive your deposit back when you close the account.

Another way to build your credit is through a credit builder loan. A credit builder loan is exactly what it sounds like. Its sole purpose it to help people build credit. The way is works is, the money that you borrow is held by the lender in an account and not released to you until the loan is repaid. I call it a forced savings program and the good thing is your payment will be recorded to the credit bureaus. To look into this type of loan, check with your credit union or community banks.

One final way to build credit is to ask for a co-signer on a loan. This is usually used when purchasing a car. But please note, even though you have a co-signer, it doesn't mean you don't have to make payments. If you miss any payments, the person who you co-signed with bares the ultimate responsibility for payment timeliness. If payments are missed, it can mess up the credit for the both of you. So if you plan on having a co-signer on your loan, make sure you make all of your payments and make them on time.

As you can see there are critical tasks to focus on when it comes to getting your credit in shape. Whatever stage you are in whether it's good credit, bad credit, or no credit, it will always take commitment and a good plan of action to not only get your credit in shape but to keep it in shape.

In regards to the importance of good credit when buying a home, I had a discussion with the CEO and founder of Credit with Chris, Mrs. Chris Bridges. Her knowledge and wisdom has helped many people in the DMV (DC, Maryland, Virginia) area understand how credit works. Her conversations about finances and credit lead me to create this chapter and for that I thank her.

As I close this chapter, I've asked Chris to say a few words...

"I want to be the first to say congratulations on getting your home. Whether it's next month or next year, if you stay focused on the promise and not the process it will happen for you. As you've learned in this book, your credit profile is the most important factor of home ownership. The reality is, if you don't you have enough cash to buy your home, you need credit to borrow someone else's. If you're wondering, what's credit got to do with it? EVERYTHING!"

For more tips on credit improvement visit
Bonus.TheVeteranHomeowner.com

HOMEBUYER'S NOTES

_____

_____

_____

_____

_____

_____

_____

_____

_____

_____

©Glasbergen
glasbergen.com

**"We're offering you an assumable mortgage.
We assume you'll make the payments and you can
assume we'll make your life miserable if you don't."**

Reprinted by permission. Drawing by Randy Glasbergen

CHAPTER 2 – THE VA LOAN

"If I were asked to name the chief benefit of the house, I should say: the house shelters day-dreaming, the house protects the dreamer, the house allows one to dream in peace."
~ Gaston Bachelard

As we began this book, we discussed how your credit is the foundation of the home buying process. After you establish your credit worthiness, it's time to consider your financing options. Between Conventional, FHA, VA, and USDA loans, I consider the VA Loan as the best way for a military veteran to buy a home. This is how I purchased my home over 20 years ago.

Before I learned about the program offered by the Veteran's administration, I truly believed it was going to take a lot of money up front for me to even consider becoming a homeowner. I would play out scenarios in my head such as: if I saved this amount for a certain number of years or if I could get a family member to give me a gift for such amount then I could be a homeowner. I tell you it really seemed overwhelming at times!

It was around 1996 when I learned from a knowledgeable real estate agent that the VA has a homebuying program that helps service members, veterans, and eligible surviving spouses become homeowners. As part of their mission to serve us, The Veteran's Association provides a home loan guaranty benefit and other housing-related programs to help you buy, build, repair, retain, or adapt a home for your own personal occupancy. The more I learned about this program, the more excited I became. I was about to own my first home and I enlisted the Veteran's Administration to help me initiate and complete my home buying mission. I have made many financial decisions over my military career but I can truly say taking advantage of the VA Loan program was my best financial decision, hands down!

VA LOAN SUMMARY

The United States VA (Veterans Affairs) Department began insuring loans for our military veterans in 1944 as part of a plan to combat the devastation and aftermath associated with the war.

The VA does not fund, nor do they approve or close VA loans themselves. The VA does however set forth the guidelines that the mortgage lenders must follow when originating VA mortgages. I wanted to mention this because I still have veterans who will ask me, "Brian, do you think I can get a loan from the VA?" So as you see, it's not the VA the gives you the loan. The VA does insure each and every loan made to our veterans which in turn makes it possible for mortgage lenders to offer veterans this amazing home financing option.

The Veteran Affairs based program has insured over 18 million home loans. It has been and still provides our military veterans with an outstanding option when purchasing a new home or even refinancing a current loan.

Purchase loans help the veterans purchase a home at competitive interest rates, often without requiring a down-payment or private mortgage insurance.

Getting the Process Started

In order to obtain a VA loan you must complete a whole list of action items. Your lender will go over each one with you, and I have also given you a "getting starting list" in chapter four. But before you get started on an intensive list of requirements, the process begins with getting pre-qualified.

Your first step will be supplying your lender with your overall financial picture to include your debt, income and assets. After evaluating this information, your lender can give you an idea of the mortgage amount for which you qualify. Pre-qualification does not have to be in person as it can be done over the phone or on the Internet. This process does *not* include an analysis of your credit report or an in-depth look at your ability to purchase a home. Also note, there are usually no costs involved. Pre-qualification is usually a quick procedure and is based on the information you provide to your lender. You need to know that even if you are pre-qualified the amount listed on paper may not be a sure thing; it's just the amount that you may be approved for.

Because of this reason, being a pre-qualified buyer doesn't carry the same weight as being a pre-approved buyer who has been more thoroughly vetted.

Let's now go over the pre-approval process. Pre-approvals tend to be much more involved. At this point you are going to complete an official mortgage application and supply the lender with the necessary documentation to perform an extensive check on your financial background and current credit rating. By completing these steps, you'll have a better idea of the specific mortgage amount you will be qualified for and the interest rate that you will be charged on a loan.

With pre-approval, you will receive a conditional commitment in writing for an exact loan amount, allowing you to look for a home at or below the stated price. Obviously, this puts you at an advantage when dealing with a potential seller, as he or she will know you're a step closer to obtaining an actual mortgage.

Getting your pre-approved status also makes it much easier for your real estate agent. He or she now has a financially vetted buyer to present to potential sellers. This will also make a difference come contract time. If a seller knows the buyer has been pre-approved by a lender, he or she also knows there is an improved chance that the deal will go to closing.

The Program Works to Your Benefit

VA Home Loans are provided by private lenders, such as banks, credit unions, and mortgage companies, and are available to military service members and their families. The VA guarantees a portion of the loan, enabling the lender to provide you with more favorable terms. The guarantee simply means the VA will reimburse the lender for any losses that may result from borrower default. The big foot stomper with this program is you as the borrower can receive 100% financing for the purchase of your new home.

(Disclaimer – Check with your lender for loan limits in your area) or visit **Bonus.TheVeteranHomeOwner.com**

I want to let you know that this is not a first time buyer only type of program. You can reuse your benefit multiple times and the VA loans are assumable as long as the person assuming the loan is qualified. Contrary to popular belief, you can even have more than one VA loan at the same time. Check with your knowledgeable VA lender for more information, requirements and details.

Inspections and Appraisals

Before guaranteeing your loan, the United States Department of Veteran Affairs (VA home loans division) wants to ensure that the home you wish to buy or sell is a worthy investment. Part of ensuring this is by performing the VA home loan inspection. This mandatory inspection is an appraisal and visual inspection combined. Its purpose is to check for any damages or defects in the home that lower its overall value or risk the safety of its occupants. This is not to be confused with the standard home inspection that is completed by a licensed home inspector.

A home inspection is not a requirement for a VA loan but it is highly recommended by the Department of Housing and Urban Development (HUD). Some states do require an inspection for termites and other wood-destroying insects, but a property inspection reviews the core items of the property.

The Process

When a contract is agreed upon between a seller and a buyer, the sales contract is forwarded to the lender who then orders a property appraisal. The appraiser's duty is to determine the subject property's current market value. This is important, so remember this. **Regardless of what the sales contract says, the VA lender will always use the lower of the sales price or appraised value when establishing a maximum loan amount.**

An appraiser will physically visit the property as well as research information for similar homes in the area and compare their sales prices with the sales price of the unit. A VA lender wants to have a marketable property as well as make sure the home will sell for a reasonable price. If there is a variance of more than 10 percent in the sales price of area homes after all adjustments are made, the final sale price can be lowered.

As far as inspections and appraisals, remember this. The property inspection evaluates the property's physical condition while the property appraisal helps establish the current market value.

Minimum Property Requirements

The VA has a list of minimum property requirements, or MPRs, that must be addressed by the appraiser and appear on the appraisal report.

- The home must be residential and not commercial and it must be occupied by the borrower.

- The property must display adequate living quarters which includes a working kitchen along with bathroom and bedroom(s).
- The property's plumbing along with its electrical systems must demonstrate to be in good working order.
- The home shall also have a working heating system along with hot water.
- The roof is an area that may be different as compared to other appraisal types as if it has more than three layers of shingles on the roof, the shingles will have to be replaced in their entirety.

The VA appraiser will also note if there are any hazardous materials on the site and that the structure shows no signs of defective craftsmanship along with deferred maintenance such as a foundation that appears cracking or even a basement that appears to be damp. As with other government-backed loans, if the home was built prior to 1978, the property must be inspected for lead-based paint and if found, the offending paint must be removed or covered with drywall or some other type of permanent repair. The VA appraisal is more extensive than other appraisals such as those performed for conventional loans underwritten to Fannie Mae or Freddie Mac guidelines. In my opinion, this is a great thing. I consider it as a much needed layer of protection. The intensity of a VA appraisal combined with a property inspection has kept potential VA borrowers from owning defective properties. These safeguards are in place to protect you and not to simply terminate a sales contract.

I know that was a lot to digest but I felt it was important that you have a working knowledge of the process. The VA appraisal process is one of the most important parts of the home buying journey because of this it is important that you work with an experienced VA lender and/or real estate agent as part of your "Success Team". Also remember to always consult with your lender or the VA directly with questions or concerns you may have.

Reminder: the VA Home Loan Inspection can help to identify potential defects in a home, but it should not be used in lieu of an actual home inspection. In my opinion, buyers should always order and pay for a separate home inspection by a licensed and professional home inspector. But of course the decision is up to you.

The VA Funding Fee

When purchasing a home using the VA home loan program you may have to pay a VA Funding Fee unless you are considered in an exempt status. The fee was created to reduce the loans cost to taxpayers considering this program requires no down payment with no monthly mortgage insurance. In short, the basic funding fee of 2.15 percent must be paid to VA by all but certain *exempt veterans*. A down payment of 5 percent or more will reduce the fee to 1.5 percent, and a 10 percent down payment will reduce it to 1.25 percent. A funding fee of 2.40 percent must be paid by all eligible Reserve/National Guard individuals. VA buyers don't have to pay the funding fee in cash. Many choose to finance it into the loan.

The following persons are exempt from paying the funding fee:

- Veterans receiving VA compensation for service-connected disabilities.
- Veterans who would be entitled to receive compensation for service-connected disabilities if they did not receive retirement pay.
- Surviving spouses of veterans who died in service or from service-connected disabilities (whether or not such surviving spouses are veterans with their own entitlement and whether or not they are using their own entitlement on the loan).

Please note that the VA has the final say on who is exempt.

Lender's Benchmarks

Per the VA there are no minimum credit score requirements when using the VA program. Instead the VA requires a lender to review the entire loan profile to make a lending decision. With that being said, most lenders are able to set their own credit score benchmarks. Applicants with scores below a lender's benchmark usually can't be approved for VA financing. That minimum will vary from lender to lender, but most VA-approved lenders, are looking for a credit score of at least 620.

As you can see, the VA home loan program offers some amazing benefits. So let's recap the features:

- No down payment unless it is required by the lender or the purchase price is more than the reasonable value for the property.
- VA rules limit the amount you can be charged for closing cost.

- Closing costs may be paid by the seller, realtor, builder, or lender.
- No private mortgage insurance (PMI) premium requirement.
- The lender can't charge you a penalty fee if you pay your loan off early.
- The VA may be able to provide you some assistance if you run into difficulty making payments.

In order to give you a complete picture of the home loan options, I included a quick summary of the FHA, Conventional and USDA Loan programs so you may have a better comparison picture.

The FHA Loan

The Federal Housing Administration (FHA) mortgage insurance program is managed by the Department of Housing and Urban Development (HUD), which is a department of the federal government. FHA loans are available to veterans and all other types of borrowers as well. The government insures the lender against losses that might result from borrower default. With this program you will be required to make a down payment as low as 3.5% of the purchase price. You will also have to pay for mortgage insurance, which will increase the size of your monthly payments. Some lenders can finance borrowers with scores of 580 and lower.

The Conventional Loan

A conventional mortgage is a home loan that isn't guaranteed or insured by the federal government and conforms to the loan limits set forth by Freddie Mac and Fannie Mae. You can get a conventional loan at a fixed or adjustable rate. Conventional loans are offered by private entities such as banks, credit unions, private lenders or savings institutions. Because the government does not guarantee them, if the buyer defaults, they're a higher risk for lenders.

Conventional loans also require a larger down payment, so those buyers tend to have a more secure financial standing and are less likely to default. The larger down payment also means lower monthly payments. Plus, with the ever-increasing mortgage insurance premiums on FHA loans, payments for conventional loans can be much more manageable in comparison. A 660 credit score is a common benchmark for conventional loans, but if you have a higher credit score it may allow you to contend for better rates and terms.

The USDA Loan

The U.S. Department of Agriculture (USDA) maintains a unique home loan program through its Rural Development office. USDA loans are the only other no-down payment loan program on the market. The home must also be located in what the USDA considers a qualified rural area. USDA purchase loans come with both an upfront guarantee fee of 2.75 percent of the loan amount and an annual mortgage insurance premium of 0.5 percent of the loan balance. A 620 credit score is often required and a borrower's income cannot exceed 115 percent of the area's median income.

So now you can see what the differences are between what are called *"the big three"* (and the USDA Loan). The choice is yours. If you have the money to put down between 3.5 percent to 20 percent, either the FHA or Conventional loan may serve you best. It's up to you to decide because at the end of the day, you are in control of your financial destiny. As you will hear me say many times throughout this book, "do your due diligence before making a final decision."

Types of Homes That Qualify

When you decide on buying a home, you have the ability to pick and choose between the VA, FHA, Conventional or USDA loan. Again, my belief is that VA loans are the most powerful and cost-effective mortgage program on the market. With that said, let's go over what type of homes qualify under the VA program.

Townhomes and Single Family detached homes are considered to be the bread and butter selection when it comes to VA qualification while some other types of homes have other requirements.

Condos

Let's start off with condos, as this is what I consider the first tier of affordability. This type of property is eligible for VA financing. However, the entire condo must receive VA approval before a buyer can obtain a loan for one particular unit.

Hopefully, the condo or condo complex that you select will have already been through the VA's approval process. Check the VA's current list of approved complexes located on **Bonus.TheVeteranHomeowner.com** or ask a lender to determine approval status. If the condo is not on the "approved" list, your lender can request approval directly from the VA. I recently heard this at an event and hopefully it comes to fruition, but the condo requirement may be going away in the near future. Cross your fingers and your toes on this one. If this does happen, I will send a direct announcement to all you that have registered on **Bonus.TheVeteranHomeowner.com**

Townhomes (These types of homes do not have to be VA approved)

Manufactured homes

These properties are better known as mobile homes. They are eligible for VA financing. However, finding a lender willing to fund a manufactured home purchase may not be easy. The reason for this is, lenders don't like depreciating properties; accordingly, they are usually hesitant to take a chance on a manufactured home. If you find a lender who is willing to work the deal, the manufactured home must meet certain criteria in order to earn VA approval:

- Must be properly affixed to a permanent foundation
- Single-wide homes must be at least 400 square feet
- Double-wide homes must be at least 700 square feet
- Homes must have permanent eating, cooking, sleeping and sanitary facilities

Modular Homes

Prefabricated homes also known as modular homes can also be financed through VA loans. The way these homes are manufactured is very interesting as they are built in sections at a factory and reassembled on-site by a contractor. Remember that I stated, "lenders don't like depreciating properties." Well the good news is modular homes are more likely to *appreciate* as compared to the manufactured homes. So with that said, it should be easier finding an accommodating lender for this type of home.

In order to qualify for a VA loan, the modular home must be attached to a permanent foundation. The home must also have been built according to HUD guidelines or receive certification from the state in which it was constructed.

New Construction

Obtaining a VA construction loan is possible, but it definitely requires some work. According to the VA, builders, plans and building sites must be VA-approved. Three different inspections are required. Builders must provide at least a one-year warranty on homes that are built. What I've noticed is some contractors are willing to build a home based on VA loan preapproval status. You wait under preapproval status until the home is complete, you then proceed to purchase the home with a regular VA loan. Assuming all goes well with the appraisal, the loan should close quickly.

Buying Land Only

This option is a no-go when it comes to VA financing. You can't use a VA loan to purchase a plot of land only unless you plan to build immediately. You may have other options, which I will cover briefing under Construction to Permanent Loans.

Construction to Permanent Loans

"Construction to Permanent Loan" is not a new program for other types of loans. For veterans, it is an option if you are able to find a VA lender that will package and approve such a deal. In general, it is a one-time closing, with up to 100% financing plus VA funding fees and no mortgage insurance. The lot can be purchased as part of the closing, or it can already be owned. At the end of construction, the loan is modified into permanent financing.

This process begins with a veteran completing the pre-approval process exactly as if they were acquiring any other VA mortgage. Once the applicant obtains approval for the purchase price along with a payment they are comfortable with, the process can begin. The next step is for the agent to find lots with or without home packages that are in the price range. As the lot shopping continues, looking at and interviewing different builders is the next very important step. Typically, these would be custom builders who have a variety of plans for homes they build. These plans can be customized for a veteran's needs. The builder can help with a budget for the square footage cost for what the veteran wants. There is also the option to build a modular home. As I mentioned earlier in this chapter, a modular home is built in a factory and shipped to the site. It can be an option that is sometimes more affordable.

> *For example, you find a lot for $100,000 and a builder that will build the home for $200,000. The veteran

would have a $300,000 purchase price and loan amount. Next comes closing and then construction starts. The most important aspect of this process is that the rate is locked prior to closing so the veteran is not playing the market by risking a higher payment.

*Examples are for reference only, every loan and customer are unique.

When the house is ready the veteran can move in. There is no other loan process or underwriting. This is what is called a true one-time close. The benefits are:

- You choose the lot and settings
- You choose house designs and style
- You choose all colors, fixtures, flooring, appliances, etc.
- Your rate is locked prior to closing
- Everything is new with a warranty so there are no repairs or replacements to start off homeownership

This program requires that the builder be accepted into the program, or must already be an approved VA Builder, or have the ability to obtain approval. The VA guidelines are the same as they would be on a normal VA purchase. The property must remain owner occupied. In other words, you can't purchase the property and treat it as rental property.

Co-ops

Co-ops are not currently eligible for VA loans. VA financing for these shared-ownership properties expired in December 2011, and at the time of this writing, have not been renewed.

As you can see, there are many options available for the VA buyer when it comes to the VA Loan. Just as there are many options when it comes to types of homes there are many more options when it comes to selecting your lender. I will discuss this in more detail in chapter four, but it's imperative that you interview your lender and ask the right questions before you proceed with such a big financial commitment.

If you need more information on lenders that provide excellent service to our Veterans go to:

Bonus.TheVeteranHomeowner.com to receive my list of resources.

The Closing Cost

I want to make sure I discussed closing cost before I ended this chapter. I didn't want you to think no money down meant no costs are associated with this the VA Home Loan program. The good news is even though costs are associated with the process, there are limits to the types of closing costs that may be paid. The closing costs are split into allowable and non-allowable closing costs. In this chapter, I will discuss them both.

There is an easy way to remember which costs you are allowed to pay. Just remember the acronym ACTORS.

(A) Appraisal
(C) Credit Report
(T) Title Insurance
(O) Origination Fee
(R) Recording Fee
(S) Survey

These are common fees which can be found on most every VA mortgage. They may vary a bit by amount but these are that can be paid for by the veteran.

Even though the VA lender requires a processing and an underwriting fee in order to approve the VA loan, the veteran may not pay for the following charges and any other fee deemed "non-allowable."

Attorney
Underwriting
Escrow
Processing
Document
Tax Service

The seller is your friend, hopefully! If the seller agrees to your offer and they want the deal to go through they must understand the part they play in the process. Those non allowable closing costs can be paid by the seller of the property. The way this is typically handled is through the sales contract. You as the buyer can say, "We'll pay you $250,000 for this home as long as you pay for $3,000 in closing costs."

Paying for the veteran's closing costs is called in a real estate transaction (a seller concession), and is limited to four percent of the sales price of the home. If a home sells for $400,000, then the seller can only pay $16,000 of the buyer's costs.

Such concessions can be used to pay for the buyer's **VA funding fee, loan costs, property taxes and insurance** among others.

Your lender can help out too...

The lender may offset part or all your closing costs with a lender credit. Lenders can offer a credit to a borrower by adjusting the borrower's interest rate. This is a good question you can ask your lender during the interview process. Will your company assist in closing cost?

As you can see those closing costs are definitely one of those nuances that stand out when it comes to the VA loan, especially with regard to who is responsible for any particular fee. Again, don't forget to consult with your lender if there are any questions about who pays for what.

HOMEBUYER'S NOTES

_____

_____

_____

_____

_____

_____

_____

_____

_____

©Glasbergen
glasbergen.com

"All we want is a cozy little cottage with a charming rose garden and a white picket fence, six bedrooms, eight bathrooms, a private tennis court and in-ground swimming pool for less than we're paying now in rent."

Reprinted by permission. Drawing by Randy Glasbergen

CHAPTER 3 – THE REAL ESTATE AGENT (YOUR BATTLE BUDDY)

"Real Estate cannot be lost or stolen, nor can it be carried away. Purchased with common sense, paid for in full, and managed with reasonable care, it is about the safest investment in the world."

~ President Franklin D. Roosevelt

A Real Estate Agent can be a Veteran's Best Friend!

Let's start off with asking the question; what is a Real Estate Agent? *Wikipedia defines the real estate broker or real estate salesperson as a person who acts as an intermediary between sellers and buyers of real estate/real property and attempts to match up sellers who wish to sell and buyers who wish to buy.* Real estate agents who represent buyers are commonly known as a buyer's agent. Real estate agents who represent sellers are commonly known as a listing agent.

When you work with a real estate agent, their fiduciary responsibility is to you but in most cases a contract has to be signed and agreed upon through exclusive agency. What does this mean? It means you have an expert who is looking out for your best financial interests, an expert who is contractually bound to do everything in their power to protect you. It's the agent making a commitment to say, we are going through this together. Let me back up and tell why a real estate agent is important. Laws change every year and vary from state to state. People purchase a new home every 7-10 years, and a lot can change between transactions. Real estate agents are immersed in real estate, and they *must* stay current with all the updates in regulations, laws, contracts and practices. Once you retain your agent, they put that knowledge to work for you. Since you are a veteran, your real estate agent needs to understand the VA Loan process and also how the veteran differs from any other customer.

Selecting Your Real Estate Agent.

If you have never purchased a home before, you may not even know a real estate agent, but it's easy to find one. Finding a real estate agent is not the issue, finding one that is qualified to work with a veteran is what's hard to find. While there is no specific license an agent needs to have in order to work with military, there is an accreditation an agent can get called MRP (Military Relocation Professional). At least with this certification, you know that you will have an agent that knows how the military operates along with knowledge about the military way of life. Another type of agent who may be a great pick for you is the real estate agent who is also a veteran. If they have purchased a home using the VA loan process that is obviously an added bonus. In order to know if an agent is the best fit for you, take the time to conduct an interview. Your agent really can make a difference between a real estate transaction that goes well and one that goes south, so it behooves you to find the right agent that will best represent you.

Interviewing Your Real Estate Agent

Before we go into interview mode I want to go over some more of what I call Real Estate Agent 101. As I mentioned earlier in this chapter, real estate agents who represent buyers are commonly known as a buyer's agent. Real estate agents who represent sellers are commonly known as a listing agent. Since we are talking about buying a home, let's look at six questions that you need to ask a real estate agent during the interview process.

1. Do you have a list of trustworthy and knowledgeable professionals?

Your buyer's agent should have several contacts in the mortgage industry that they can recommend to you. As you can figure out so far, all real estate agents are not created equally and all mortgage companies and consultants are not created equally either. When buying a home you will likely need a title attorney (also known as a title company), a home inspector, insurance agent (for your home owner's insurance), and other professional real estate industry professionals. Also don't be afraid to ask the potential buyer's agent if he or she has a list of professionals they can provide to you.

2. How long have you been a licensed real estate agent?

Experience in the real estate industry is important. But what is also important is if the agent works with a broker who is knowledgeable of the veteran home buying process. A good broker will make sure his or her agents are well equipped for success. The industry rule of thumb is the longer a real estate agent has been selling real estate, the more transactions they have likely completed. But in the case of our veterans, the question is: how many veterans have you represented in the home buying process?

3. Is real estate your full-time career or a part-time job?

Buying a home is a time consuming process. As a potential homebuyer you have a job, family, and other responsibilities. It's important that your buyer's agent is available based on your time, so the consensus is you need to select a full time agent. I believe if you select an agent and he or she is knowledgeable and has a good support staff working with him, then it's okay to select that part time agent. If you come across an agent this is part-time or as the industry calls them, Dual Career agents, ask him or her how they plan to support you based on the limited availability they may have. So if you really like this agent and he or she is considered dual career, figure out a way to make your partnership a win-win team. But if having a dual career agent is not what you want to use, feel free to select an agent based on what suits you best.

4. Do you have a list of testimonials or past clients?

Every buyer's agent should be able to provide you with a list of testimonies. If the agent is doing a great job then it should be noted for the public to see. There are some industry websites that will allow you to access various agents and to see testimonies from past clients and customers.

For a list of these websites go to
Bonus.TheVeteranHomeowner.com.

5. Do you have real estate agent website?

A website is a great place to learn about not only the potential buyer's agent but also about the local neighborhoods, schools, and also find some helpful testimonials. The website should also allow you to do a preliminary search on properties in your desired area.

6. What type of technology do you use for assisting your clients in the home buying process?

This question is very important in the age of improved technology. Does your agent have the technology to automatically send you listings based on your criteria and is the information current and up to date? Are they able to walk you through different technologies in order to find your desired home based on your criteria? What will they use to transmit data outlining homes in your select area?

These are a few of the important questions to ask during your initial consultation as it established how committed your agent will be to your home buying success. Interviewing your agent will hopefully increase your comfort level when it comes to making your decision. The agent who will represent you must be well versed on the process when it comes to the VA Loan program. There are unique nuances that require knowledge, and experience. Remember, as you go through your transaction, your agent is going to be your right hand man or woman, or as it's called in the Army, your Battle Buddy! Selecting your real estate agent in not an easy thing to do. You have to make sure they know their stuff. It's important to do your research and don't forget to ask for references.

HOMEBUYER'S NOTES

©Glasbergen
glasbergen.com

REAL ESTATE

"The seller will accept your downpayment of 5,000 returnable beer and soda bottles, providing one of those bottles contains a check for thirty-five thousand dollars."

Reprinted by permission. Drawing by Randy Glasbergen

CHAPTER 4 – ENLISTING THE LENDER

"I wonder if it will be—can be—any more beautiful than this,' murmured Anne, looking around her with the loving, enraptured eyes of those to whom 'home' must always be the loveliest spot in the world, no matter what fairer lands may lie under alien stars."

~ L. M. Montgomery, *Anne of the Island*

When it comes to finding a lender, this is something that should take time and due diligence. When I was searching for my home I didn't get a chance to search for many options when it came to a lender. My deal was a little different as I went to a builder and purchased what was called (A Builder's Closeout) and fortunately the builder had a lender who already knew the VA process plus the builder's preselected lender paid all of my closing. What I didn't know at the time was you don't have to select the lender the builder provides, you can bring your very own lender to the deal. For us military folks, we can always go to one of the banks we frequent that has some sort of military affiliations. I like these lenders as they understand the military as far as finances and benefits, such a Base Allowance for Housing (BAH) and other special pays. There are also many other lenders out there who may be able to offer special deals on top of the VA loan.

It's not always easy to find a mortgage lender. Gather a few rate quotes, and then follow up with some research and interviews before you choose the lender who is right for you. You can of course go online to get an idea, but remember, rates change daily. If you see bank A has a great rate today, don't be surprised if bank B and C both have better rates tomorrow. Also I believe one of the best ways to find a lender is by asking family, friends and co-workers. Don't be afraid to ask your co-worker, "Who did you use as your lender when you purchased your home?" Also ask them why they selected that particular lender. Prepare to take notes as the process of finding a lender has begun.

A good lender can qualify you for a loan and offer advice on ways to improve your credit and should talk to you about mortgage payments in context with the rest of your financial plan. At this point you should have already selected a real estate agent. He or she can also give you some recommendations based on experience with various lenders. Selecting the right lender is very important, as lenders are a big part of the first offensive wave during your real estate purchase mission.

Interviewing Your Lender

Buying a home is an exciting thing as homeownership is part of what is called "The American Dream." But in order to achieve this part of the "American Dream" you must find the right lender. Let me back up, I know I will be talking about interviewing a lender but I also realize that not everyone needs a lender; some folks may use cash only. But for this chapter of the book we are only going to discuss those who need to take out a loan. When selecting a lender you need one that is well versed in making sure *you*, "the military veteran" is getting the best loan available.

As veterans, we have access to arguably the most powerful mortgage option on the planet, but this is the sad part of the story. One in three home buying veterans don't know that they have a home loan benefit. If you are dealing with a lender that isn't versed in the VA loan process, they may not present this benefit to you as an option. It's not totally up to the lender to ask if you are currently in or have ever served in the military. It's up to you to share this information with the lender. While I am writing this book, I have learned of legislation that is in the process of being passed that will ask you on the loan application, "Have you served in the military?" But until this is fully enacted, the first question I would ask the lender would be, *Do you service VA loans*? If they answer with a delay or say something like, "Well we don't like to do those types of loans," then that is your invitation to leave. And here is a foot stomper; *you don't have to apply for a loan to ask questions*. You can find out a lot by simply calling to ask about a lender's loan programs. If the loan officer is hard to reach or gives you a hard sell in regard to other types of loans, you may not want to work with that lender.

I want to warn you about lender speak. This is the language they use which is full of acronyms and bank only teams such as; APRs, ARMs, balloons, points, buy downs and many more terms which the average veteran homebuyer would have no clue when it comes to the definitions. My suggestion is for you to ask Mr. or Ms. Lender if they can explain all of this to you in a language where you can understand what each option means for you, not just for today but for the long term. You also need to find someone who will agree to set expectations upfront, including how long the loan process will take, how often the two of you will communicate, and to include your preferred means of communication such as by email or phone.

Another way you can vet your lender is through lender reviews. One of the easiest ways to check for any negative comments or reassuring statements is to check the Internet. When in doubt, Google it out! Also don't forget your friends at the Better Business Bureau *(BBB.org)*.

One of the most important questions is about turnaround time as mortgage loans have a tendency to get delayed. So don't be afraid to ask, "What is your average turnaround time?" Turnaround is the time it takes to close a mortgage loan and it varies with the type of mortgage, buyer/homeowner situations, and lender processing efficiency. A good rule of thumb is to assume that a typical mortgage loan will take around four to six weeks to close from application date.

I would even recommend asking who will service your loan because if your loan will be sold, it may be more difficult to track someone down later who can help you with any issues. This is something that I remember very well as my first loan was with a small lender out of Maryland and within two months after the closing the loan was sold to one of those big lenders who eventually went out of business during the finance debacle of 2008.

Another few things you can ask are: what happens if the appraisal comes in to low? What happens if my rate lock expires before closing? How do you handle those problems that may happen at the last minute?

The interview process should not just be made up of one-way communication. It should go both ways, as the lender should ask questions in return about long-term plans for homeownership and overall financial goals. You want someone who focuses on you, and not just on your loan.

We have been focusing on interviewing the lender but I wanted to share another foot stomper with you. A lender may ask you in the interview process to provide your SSN in order to pull your credit. DO NOT and I mean DO NOT allow lenders to pull your credit report before you have chosen a lender. Multiple inquiries can negatively affect your credit score, potentially costing you a lower rate. Once you have chosen a mortgage company, you will authorize them to pull your credit report as part of the application process. Okay, now that I got that off of my chest, let's continue with the lender selection process.

Selecting the lender

When selecting your lender it's important to know they do not have to be local. You may live in Florida and your lender may be in Fairfax, Virginia. With the power of faxing, email and even electronic signatures, the process of getting things done is much easier than it was 20 years ago.

The main thing is for you feel comfortable with the information provided and knowledgeable while going through the process. OK, it's time for you to go select your lender. Don't forget to get all of their contact info to include: email, cell phone, fax number, file sharing account, websites and anything else you can think of in order to stay in touch and keep the flow of communication going.

Preparing for what is needed

Now that you have selected your lender you will need to find what's needed to get your mission underway. Your lender may have more requirements than what I am showing below, but at least it will be enough to get you started.

Let's begin with personal information such as:

_____ Name, address, and phone number (work and cell)

_____ Previous addresses (from past 2 years)

_____ Social Security numbers for all
(Only provide after you select your lender)

_____ Date of birth

_____ Copy of Valid ID such as driver's license or passport

_____ State where you plan to purchase your new home

_____ Number and age of dependents

Let's start gathering your military information:

_____ A Copy of your DD214 (if separated or retired from the military)

_____ Completed Request for Certificate for Eligibility (COE) *form 26-1880

_____**State of Service from your commanding officer

You need to provide Employment and Income data

_____ Name, address, phone number and dates of employment for all employers over the last 2 years

_____ Leave and Earning Statement (Current Month)

_____ W-2 from the previous tax year

_____ 1099R if receiving a military retirement

_____ Copy of social security, VA disability award letters (if you receive this type of income)

_____ (If divorced), copy of divorce decree and settlement paperwork

The COE is not something you can go at alone. You will need the assistance of your new lender. They will walk you through your request and make sure you get the certificate in a timely manner. For information on how to retrieve form 26-1880 visit the Veterans Administration at

http://www.benefits.va.gov/homeloans/purchaseco_certificate.asp

**this is a requirement if you are still on active duty*

_____ If self-employed: Last 2 years tax returns with all the applicable schedules

Don't forget your assets

_____ Banks statement for all checking and savings accounts (60 days' worth)

_____ Investment account statements (if requested)

_____ Real estate Income (if applicable)

Gather this data is part of the preplanning process. The lender may not need every item on this checklist or they may need more but either way, you are going to have a good jump start.

By the way, I am repeating this foot stomper, *DO NOT and I mean DO NOT allow lenders to pull your credit report before you have chosen a lender*. Multiple inquiries can negatively affect your credit score, potentially costing you a lower rate. Once you have chosen a mortgage company, you will authorize them to pull your credit report as part of the application process.

The lender plays a very important role when it comes to buying your home. It's important to find the right one in order to experience home buying success.

HOMEBUYER'S NOTES

"It's a very historic location. This house
is located on the very same planet
where Elvis Presley was born!"

Reprinted by permission. Drawing by Randy Glasbergen

CHAPTER 5 – DECIDING ON YOUR BASECAMP

"Owning a home is the culmination of many years of hard work and the realization of the American Dream."

~ Solomon Ortiz

There are some key things to consider before you begin to look at the first home. If you are currently on active duty you may want to be somewhere close to where you are assigned, especially if you are on a recall roster. Depending on what part of the country you plan on living in, you may have to consider the traffic. Here in what we call the DMV (DC, Maryland Virginia) area, depending on where you live it may take you one to two hours to get home while sitting in rush hour traffic. Now if you live pretty close to your assignment then traffic can become more manageable. The truth is that traffic is a major concern for most people but this is just one of many things to consider. As you look into where to buy your home it's also a good idea to consider what you like to do for recreation and hobbies. Are you someone who likes to be close to the water? Do you like to be near biking trails? Remember you may work Monday through Friday but on the weekend, it's time to let your hair down and have fun. Let's not forget about the family.

If you have kids you don't want to keep them out of the process. Think about what school you want them to go to and if you want them to walk or ride a bus. Your decision on where to live is a decision to be made by all the people under your roof.

Your home price and the budget

When I started looking for a home for my family, we initially got caught up in all sorts of charming features but we decided to keep our priorities list close at hand in order to help us stay on track. Staying on track equals staying within your budget. I recall talking to a friend about how the home buying process went for her and how frustrated she became when all this extra pricing appeared on her home order just because she tried to duplicate the builder's model. The price on the sign said, "Starting in the Low $300,000s" but when she added up the final cost, it came to nearly $400,000. Talk about sticker shock! Here is a problem that I have noticed when going into some of these model homes. You get exposed to upgraded everything. Do you like the wood floors, guess what, that's an upgrade! How about those granite counter tops? Those are upgrades too! Oh yeah, did you see that beautiful basement. Yeah, that could be an upgrade too. Like I always tell my friends, "Don't do it", especially when it comes to staying within your budget. If you are looking at a home in a new home community I highly suggest you bring your battle buddy a.k.a. Mr. or Mrs. Real Estate agent with you. Not only will your real estate agent be your primary point of contact but he or she will also be your trusted home buying advisor.

When you are setting up your homebuying budget, the amount of money you want to spend must be within your workable monthly mortgage amount. Let me give you an example based on the Fort Meade area using 2016 numbers. A home around $250,000 will cost you around $1600 per month, and that's including taxes and insurance and an interest rate around 3.5 percent. If your budget is $2000 per month that $1600 will work for you leaving you money for other things like an emergency fund. The other thing to consider if you are on active duty is your BAH (Base Allowance for Housing), which is based on your rank and your dependent status. That amount will also assist you in determining your homebuying budget. You may want to stay within your BAH amount or slightly over. The amount you pay for your mortgage depends on you and your current financial situation. So let's discuss recommended amounts to spend on your mortgage based on percentages. This is called your debt to income ratio.

Your debt-to-income ratio (DTI) is all your monthly payments divided by your gross monthly income. This number is one way lenders measure your ability to manage the payments you make every month to repay the money you have borrowed.

To calculate your debt-to-income ratio, you add up all your monthly payments and divide them by your gross monthly income. Your gross monthly income is generally the amount of money you have earned before your taxes and other deductions are taken out. For example, if you pay $1500 a month for your mortgage and another $100 a month for an auto loan and $400 a month for the rest of your debts, your monthly debt payments are $2000. ($1500 + $100 + $400 = $2,000.) If your gross monthly income is $6000, then your debt-to-income ratio is 33 percent. ($2000 is 33% of $6000.)

Evidence from studies of mortgage loans suggests that borrowers with a higher debt-to-income ratio are more likely to run into trouble making monthly payments. The 43 percent debt-to-income ratio is important because, in most cases, that is the highest ratio a borrower can have and still get a Qualified Mortgage.

The Department of Veterans Affairs mortgage guidelines state that 41 percent is the maximum debt-to-income ratio for a military mortgage borrower. However, because of residual income, applicants whose DTI exceed 41 percent can be granted an exception.

So now you have it! Work the numbers in order to make sure your monthly expenses will not leave you in a situation that I call "house broke." Save your money for other goals in life, such as retirement, college funds and vacation.

Before we close out on the topic of setting the homeowner's budget, it's imperative that I discuss what most people don't talk about, and that is what happens when the house breaks. It's could be easy to keep the picture rosy and tell you everything is going to be just fine in regard to the house and nothing will ever, ever break, but I can't sit here and tell you something that may not end up being true. When I purchased my home, the first thing I added to my "must have list" was a home warranty program. I knew it was just an amount of time before the warranty on my various appliances expired and repairs needed to be made. If you buy, know that you're committed to years of fixing anything that breaks in the house. So with this in mind make sure your budget is set up to account for repairs. Even if you have a home warranty not every item will be covered.

Learn how to make your selection based on your style

While you are looking for your house, make sure it matches the style that you planned for. You should write each thing out that appeals to you. If you like sitting next to a fireplace on a cold winter night, you would want to make sure you have at least one fire place in your home. What about making sure the kids have a bathroom separate from yours? When I tell you this, believe me the kids will need their own space. The interior sections of the home are a good place to start when it comes to writing down what you want in advance. For example, 4 bedrooms, 2 ½ baths, big kitchen with wood floors and granite countertops and, oh yeah, you may want to add a finished basement into the mix. Now that we talked about the inside of the home let's move on to what most people notice first and that's the outside. The outside of the house creates what is called curb appeal. This is where you decide what's important at first glance. Is it the little tree in the front yard? Is it the idea of a light post next to the driveway? Decisions, decisions, decisions...

For some people who have multiple cars, it's always an idea to have a multiple car garage, but only if you plan on using it for something other than storage space. When planning for that special house, also consider, what color you want and if not a certain color, how about a brick front or brick all the way around. I always say planning helps make your decisions easier. Even if it takes drawing the house you have in your mind out on paper.

You may think what I am taking about is something that doesn't work. But I believe if you put your goals down on paper and you take action to get the things that you want, it's a good chance that you will receive the very house of your heart's desire.

Spacing for your place

Have you ever moved into a home or into an apartment only to find out you don't have enough space to put everything? Your living room set doesn't fit into the living room? That's not going to work. Let's move out of the living room and go upstairs into the bedroom. You have a California king bed, a sofa, two end tables and a big nightstand. You thought the master bedroom was big enough to fit all of your beautiful furniture. Well, it can fit but it's going to be really tight. So with all of that said, I strongly suggestion you know the measurements from the current home you live in. Determine the total square feet in your home and more importantly in the room with the most furniture.

Sometimes when you don't have enough room in the house that you absolutely love, you are going to have to make a decision. Can you say, "Yard sale, flea market or donations?" Most people have way too much stuff in their house and at some point, it's a good time to get right of things. I need you to trust me on this, and this is why. When you move into your home that is just right as far as size and dimensions, you are going to find other things to add over time, so why not make room before you even move in.

Types of homes available to purchase

When I started looking for a home, I was amazed at the many types of home that were available. It's more than saying, "I want to buy a home." Each home has a certain name based on its style. You have apartment style homes that are structured as condominiums. You also have homes that are attached to others and they are called townhomes or rowhomes depending on where you live. I grew up in Baltimore City, and if you look around the downtown area, you will see attached homes with a small or non-existent front yard. These homes have been called rowhomes for over 150 years. Also, we have homes in Baltimore that are attached with nice size front yards and these are called townhomes. I know I just confused you right? Yes, it's very confusing unless you live in Baltimore. Ok, enough shout outs for my city. Home types may vary from city to city, state to state.

The specific home style that you want should already be in your head. It may be a beautiful colonial with a large yard, which will give your children plenty of room to play. You may want a rancher style home so you don't have to run up and down stairs. Consult with your real estate agent about the type of homes that are available in your area. Let him/her assist you in selecting the best home that is within your pre-approved price range and budget.

HOMEBUYER'S NOTES

©Glasbergen
glasbergen.com

"It's the perfect home for a couple who can't decide what they want. It's a victorian split-level colonial ranch mobile cabin!"

Reprinted by permission. Drawing by Randy Glasbergen

CHAPTER 6 – DECISIONS – NEW OR USED

"We shape our dwellings, and afterwards our dwellings shape us."

~ Sir Winston Churchill

Over the years, I have heard many reasons why someone should buy new construction compared to a preexisting/used home, but the argument goes both ways. I want to give you some pros and cons on both sides of the fence.

Should you purchase a newly constructed home

When it comes to buying what the home buying industry calls, "new construction", there are some items that stand out. For me, I remember that new home smell. There was nothing like it. Walking into your home after a long day of work and enjoying the smell of your labor. Along with the new home smell is your ability to design your home just as you like it from picking out cabinets, flooring, appliances and fixtures.

Your new home can reflect your style and not someone else's taste.

Designing your home your way

Another good point when it comes to buying new construction, is you pick out the best floor plan the fits your needs. You may want to have your master bedroom on the first floor with huge walk in closets. Inside of your master suite you may desire a sitting room and a fireplace that is displayed on both sides of the wall. If you want to have a man cave or a ladies' den, you can do this and more with new construction.

Consider the Energy and Cost Savings

In today's new homes, energy efficiency is a selling factor. Compared to a home that was built twenty years ago and even five years ago, new home construction is in most cases, a better way to go. In older homes you may have those drafty, energy-wasting, single-pane windows, while in many new homes the builder will offer double or even triple-pane windows. Special window coatings and inert gases between the layers of glass are often available, saving you even more energy and money in both heating and cooling season. In fact, a 2016 survey by the National Association of Home-builders found that 90 percent of respondents listed Energy Star appliances as an essential or desirable feature in their most-wanted list.

Safety first

When you purchase new construction, you also have an added safety factor included in when it comes to your electrical systems. Most new homes are now built with state-of-the-art circuit breakers. Even today's garage door openers have advanced technology features to include infrared beams that stop the movement of the garage door if a tricycle or child is too close. Your family can even breathe easier as the cabinets, carpets, and paints now have fewer volatile compounds. Speaking of breathing, your new high-efficient furnace and air conditioners are using the latest environmentally friendly coolants.

The last feature I wanted to mention was that your home is move in ready once the building process is complete. All of your selections have been made, installed and prepped especially for you. There is no need to plan on changing out the old ceramic tiles with wood flooring or putting in new facets in the bathroom and kitchen. You are done and ready to plant some flowers in the yard and relax.

The pre-existing home has its advantages

As I always tell people, there are always two sides of the story. When it comes to homeownership and selecting new versus old, you have to make the best decision that works for you. Now I will tell you, when buying a newly constructed home, those extra options are not all free. You may end up paying thousands of dollars more than the base price, depending on what the builder includes as a bonus. That's another good reason to know what you want in your house before you go shopping. If you know that you want a four bedroom home with three baths, finished basement, wood floors throughout, updated kitchen and bathrooms, a fireplace in the family room and a sitting room in the master bedroom, then you can go looking for exactly that. As a matter of fact, you should share your requirements or wants with your battle buddy a.k.a. your real estate agent. Here is a good suggestion for those of you wanting a home that is not too old. Go to one of those new home communities that's maybe six months to a year old. There is a good chance you will find a few of those homes on the market at a price that is lower than the price you would pay for new construction with added options. Plus, I will tell you a secret. Sometimes you can get a newly constructed home that was ordered by a customer and for some reason or the other they couldn't go through with the deal. Maybe the financing fell through or something happened that canceled the contract. What does this mean for you? You have a potential home reduced for quick sale, and it is move in ready. If you like the options the customer ordered and it's your preplanned home-style, put in a contract and make that house yours. You can be in a new home at a great price in 30 to 45 days.

Let's say you don't mine purchasing a home that is 5, 10 or even 20 years or older. This is going to require you to do your due diligence. Your pre-planned options will guide you to a nice home but again and I can't say it enough, you must know what you want before you go on your home buying mission. Let's say you find an older home and it's full of character and a great design. The decision process begins as you notice that this house is in the need of some upgrades. The kitchen has linoleum floors and the cabinets are of a basic grade. The master bathroom looks good but again, those floors look like they were put down when the house was built. You fall in love with the massive master bedroom on the first floor to include the very spacious walk in closet. At this point you may say to yourself, "This home is nice but it is in need of some work." You consider the upgrades required and you figure you can accomplish the work over time. This house is priced below market value and the seller is very motivated to make a deal. In this case, the house can be yours with the right negotiator assisting you with the contract. Again, that is why it's important to have the knowledgeable real estate agent by your side.

Home Warranty Protection

Let me also add this very important option to the equation. You just never know what's gonna break when you live in an older home. Maybe I should re-phrase this to say it's not a matter of just "what" is gonna break, it's "when" is something gonna break. I have a home warranty contract and it has really come in handy over the years. I've had pipes burst, a water heater go bad, a water pump in my washing machine malfunction, a refrigerator act up, and I even had my AC unit go bad due to an issue with the compressor. Now, I could have probably gone to YouTube and figured out how to fix all of those problems, but I don't have the time. It was easier for me to pay a $75 deductible and let a repair company do the work. I can tell you my home warranty has paid for itself. So, if you ask me do I suggest you buy a home warranty with an older home, I will say absolutely. I would even go as far as suggesting that you buy one for your new home after the manufacture's warranties end. Sometimes when you are looking at an older home, the seller might sweeten the pot by throwing a homeowner's warranty in with the deal. Either way, it's definitely something for you to think about. Also keep in mind that if this house needs too much work and may be considered unsafe, the VA may not approve it for purchase using a VA loan. For more guidance, refer to my resource page in order see the VA Purchase guidelines at **Bonus.TheVeteranHomeowner.com**

A Home Inspection is not required but...

I mentioned this in Chapter two, but it bears repeating... the VA does not require a home inspection, however I highly require you look into getting one. This applies to a new or preexisting home. According to Glen Blanc of Pro-Spex Professional Home Inspection Services, "whether it's a newly built home, a resale or a fixer upper, your purchase in many instances will be the most valuable investment you will make in their lifetime. Given this fact, a detailed home inspection can provide context for that investment and aid you in making decisions as your home buying transaction moves forward."

Begin with the end in mind

When it comes to buying a home, you need to put together your exit plan. I am saying this statement for those who plan on someday selling their home. It's my opinion that many people don't include this in the preplanning phase of house hunting. When it's time to sell a home, Mr. and Mrs. Homeowner may have many questions that could have been answered with proper preplanning at the purchase stage of the process. Let me walk you through my train of thought. When you select a home to buy, think about your buyers. Yes, I mean your buyers! This is going to be the man, women or couple with kids that will fall in love with your residence at first sight. So now that I have you on this train of thought let's begin with the home selling possibilities. What if a couple with kids wants your home? What kind of things will appeal to them inside and outside of the house? Does your home have a big back yard? Are the extra bedrooms roomy? Is this home in close proximity to schools? What if it's a single first-time homeowner? Is the home in a low crime area or will you need bars on the windows? Do you have public transportation nearby? Do you get the idea? Of course you can't please everyone. Some people who come to see your newly listed home may want what you don't have and that's just part of the game. All you can do is plan on both ends of the process and hope for the best.

Of course you get to make the ultimate decision when it comes to new or used homebuying, but hopefully this chapter made you think along with taking the time to list out your very own pros and cons. When it comes to each potential home on your list, your preplanning and due diligence will help you select the home that's right for you.

HOMEBUYER'S NOTES

_____

_____

_____

_____

_____

_____

_____

_____

_____

REAL ESTATE

©Glasbergen
glasbergen.com
GLASBERGEN

"The seller has agreed to lower the price and they are willing to tear down the wall in the back yard. Ready to make an offer, Mr. Dumpty?"

Reprinted by permission. Drawing by Randy Glasbergen

CHAPTER 7 – THE CONTRACT

"There is no place more delightful than one's own fireplace."

~ **Marcus Tullius Cicero**

When you think of a contract you think of an agreement of some sort between two or more parties. The first big contract you may have completed was on the day you signed your life over to Uncle Sam. This was the day that changed your life forever. You signed a contract between yourself and your selected service to serve a certain amount of years (Term of Enlistment). After your contract was signed, you then did some other administrative duties before preparing to be shipped off to Basic Military Training (BMT). Of course if you joined ROTC in college or went to one of the service academies, your route may have been a little different from the above example, but you get the idea. But at the end of the day a contract is just a written or spoken agreement, especially one concerning employment, sales, or tenancy that is intended to be enforceable by law.

When it comes to your real estate purchase, contracts are not always the easiest documents to comprehend. The important thing to remember is if you have any questions when it comes to your contract, don't be afraid to ask your real estate agent to explain them to your satisfaction. If you still don't fully understand your contract you can enlist the help of a real estate attorney. Remember, buying a home may be your biggest investment, so it definitely requires you to be on your Ps and Qs.

The Who, What, and Why of the Earnest Money Deposit

Before I get too deep into the contract I wanted to answer questions that you probably have when it comes to the earnest money deposit.

As a prospective buyer, you are usually expected to provide what is called an earnest money deposit when you are making an offer on a home.

The deposit is returned to you if the contract is legitimately cancelled. If you opt not to buy a house without meeting the terms of the contract, you could very well risk losing your deposit. However, your contract will usually include contingencies that must be met by a specific date. If any contingencies are not satisfied, your deposit should be returned.

The earnest money deposit is an important part of the home buying process as it tells the seller that you are serious when it comes to buying their home.

When I purchased my home as a veteran, the whole earnest money thing was pretty clear but what I didn't know was how much should I put down. I was told I didn't have to put anything down as a veteran, but by putting something down, it showed good faith to the seller.

So that lead to the question of how much should I put down. I've learned the amount of money you will put down as earnest money deposit will depend on a few factors, and will vary according to your area, and is based on the price of the home you're considering. The best way to determine your amount is to talk to an experienced real estate agent. Your earnest money deposit could range anywhere from a couple hundred dollars to a few thousand. So much depends on the specific property, the competitiveness of the market and other market-specific factors.

A competitive market might mean you'll need to put down more money. A competitive market is a market where homes are selling fast. The buyers are in a competition where whoever has the most attractive offer wins and that could mean a nice size earnest money deposit or even paying full price for the listing. Most agents agree that buyers should include an earnest money amount that will be taken seriously, but not so much that a buyer's finances are at risk. It's unlikely that you'll lose your earnest money deposit, but it's important to protect yourself. So to give you a ballpark figure on how much you should expect to put down, normally 1 percent to 2 percent of the total purchase price is expected. Again, consult with your real estate agent before making your final decision.

Example: Home listed at $400,000 x 1% EMD is $4000

The benefits of a contract

Remember this, there are so many people out there in the world who are just waiting to take advantage of you in any way possible. They don't care if you're a military veteran or the CEO of a fortune 500 company. There are many scam artists just waiting for you to walk through their door. One of the most important words I learned in the military was *vigilance* and when it comes to contracts, that word definitely applies.

Before I talk about the benefits I need to tell you that a contract can be in written or verbal form, but when it comes to the purchase of real estate your contract will be a written agreement.

Now that I got that out of the way, let's discuss benefits.

1. It creates a visible record

This is important in the event that the other party wants to renege on the deal. With a contract you can reference the exact wording as stated.

Example:

> I, Mr. John E. Jones agree to pay Mr. Jerry D. Snuffy $1,500 on May 1st 2017 for the services rendered.
>
> Signed by John E. Jones Dated 2/1/17
>
> Signed by Jerry D. Snuffy Dated 2/1/17

So if Mr. Jones does not pay Mr. Snuffy his $1500 on May 1st, then Mr. Jones may have a problem.

2. Makes the agreement clear from the outset

There is no guessing involved when the contract has been made. I like to say it eliminates the "He said, She said" factor!

3. Reduces the risk of a dispute outlining timeframes and work to be performed under the contract

You know what you have to do based on your agreement, and you know when it has to be done. One of the most important sayings when it comes to real estate contracts is the phrase, "Time is of the essence." In other words, there are certain line items that must be completed by a certain date and if they are not accomplished the contract can be rendered null and void.

4. Specifies how either party can end the contract before the task is completed

In a good contract you will notice that if the services rendered are not completed by a certain date or based on specifications, the other party may not have to pay. The example I showed in the previous instance was not as thorough as it could have been. What if Mr. Snuffy doesn't provide the service by a specified date? Then guess what, Mr. Jones should not have to pay. That should be common sense right? But with deals and contracts, you have to be specific and direct. Do not leave anything up to someone else's interpretation or explanation.

Who Does the Contract Represent

The contract represents you as the buyer but it also represents the other party known as the seller. It's a two or more party agreement. This is why I said it's important to understand each contract item sentence-by-sentence and line-by-line when it comes to a real estate contract. If the seller has a certain clause in the contract, which states you must have financing approval by a certain date and your lender doesn't provide it, the seller can get out of the deal and move on. You, on the other hand, have things that the seller must adhere to according to the contract and if they don't comply you can say goodbye to the deal as well.

I think the best way for you to see how the contract represents both parties is to show an example of what happens when you submit an offer for the home you want to buy. That special home meets all of your expectations and you tell your real estate agent, "I want to put an offer on this house!" The next thing the real estate agent does is pull out the appropriate residential sales contract for your state. In that contract, two main parties are going to be introduced to the contract and they are Mr. and/or Ms. Buyer and Mr. and/or Ms. Seller. After the parties are introduced, certain items are stated such as the date of the offer, the proper legal description which should include city and state, purchase price, payment terms and date of settlement, along with the area called financing. In the financing section (as seen by my example) you will notice how both parties have a part in the success or failure of the deal.

The Buyer's *(You) obligation to purchase the Property is contingent upon the Buyer obtaining a written commitment for the loan secured by the property under some form of financing or other (such as cash) and if a financing commitment is not obtained by the buyer with a certain amount of days from the date of contract acceptance, **the seller** at seller's election and upon written notice to Buyer may declare this contract null and void and no further legal effect.*

As you can see from that example, the contract is an agreement between two or more parties where both parties are indeed represented.

The contents of the real estate contract

The items in your contract vary state to state. In order to know what's in your state's real estate contract contact your real estate agent. But in order to give you an idea of what may be found in your contract, I've listed some of the items that I am familiar with. Among these items are pages and pages worth of terms and conditions to which both parties have agreed. *Again for a detailed listing of items from your state, contact your real estate agent.*

- Date of Offer
- Buyer and Seller's Name
- Property location
- Estate Status (as in Fee Simple or Ground Rent)
- Purchase Price (the price the buyer is willing to pay, also known as the offering price)
- Payment (As in Earnest Money Deposit amounts)
- Date the sale will be finalized ("Settlement")
- Financing Option (this is where you select VA Loan)
- Home Inspection (Optional Contingency)
- Date the buyer will move in ("take possession")
- Inclusions (items to be included in the sale, such as carpeting, lighting fixtures, appliances and so forth)
- Exclusions (items not included in the sale that the buyer might otherwise expect to be, such as a fixture that the seller has negotiated to take along)

- Guarantee that the seller will provide clear title to the home, through an abstract of title, certificate of title, or title insurance policy
- Federal Lead Based Paint Law information
- Date of Contract Acceptance (This may or not be the same as the Date of Offer)

Contingencies are part of the deal

Contingencies are a very important part of the real estate process. These are the items in a contract that can make the deal a go or no go.

Your real estate contract may contain several contingencies that must be met in order for the sale to proceed. Both you (the buyer) and the seller will likely want to add various contingencies in order to protect your own interests. These contingencies often include:

- The buyer hiring a home inspector and being satisfied with the results of the resulting home inspection report
- The buyer successfully obtaining a mortgage loan or other financing
- The buyer selling his or her current house, and/or
- The seller successfully finding another house to move into.

If the contingencies outlined in the contract are not met, for example, you are turned down for a bank loan, the seller can cancel the contract and you will get a refund of your earnest money deposit. That goes back to the contingent on financing clause.

In the event of a dispute between buyer and seller on the matter of contingencies, you would have to turn to a dispute resolution process specified in the contract. An arbitrator, mediator, or small claims court judge would then decide the matter according to the provisions of the contract.

As you can see, the contract is the most important part of the real estate purchasing process. That is why it's important for you to have people on your team that truly understand the process. You must have a good real estate agent on your team who is familiar with your state approved residential contracts of sale, federal law and regulations along with any local addendum that may apply to the area where you are planning to purchase your new home.

When I purchased my home I asked many questions of my agent and the lender, as I wanted to make sure I was on the right path to homeownership success.

HOMEBUYER'S NOTES

©Glasbergen
glasbergen.com

REAL ESTATE

"This house has a great location! If you own a really good pair of shoes, it's within walking distance of Disneyland, Cape Cod, the Grand Canyon, Mall of America, and Carnegie Hall!"

Reprinted by permission. Drawing by Randy Glasbergen

CHAPTER 8 – BUYER BEWARE

"A man travels the world over in search of what he needs and returns home to find it."

~ George Moore

Now that you are out looking for your perfect home, there are a few things you need to be aware of. Everything you see is not what it seems. The best way to prepare yourself is by doing your due diligence. Do me a favor and remember these words, Caveat Emptor. These are the Latin words for "Buyer Beware". When it comes to homebuying the whole process requires you to put on your designer *Caveat Emptor* eyewear. Whether you're selecting a new home from a builder or a pre-existing home from a wonderful family who is very motivated to move, you have to go into the deal with both eyes wide open.

New Home Builder – Reputation and Reviews

This is where your investigation begins, especially when it comes to new homebuilders. Just because it looks good on the pictures and the model looks exquisite, that doesn't mean you are going to get a quality home.

When it comes to new homebuilders, you may have a small company that only builds locally or a big well-known builder with a national footprint. Before you select either one, you have to do your due diligence. Failure on the part of a builder to build you a quality home should not be an option.

Here are my suggestions to help you through the new homebuilder selection process.

After you've thought about the style of home you want, you can create a list of potential builders in your area. You can find that list based on the city and state you live in by registering on **Bonus.TheVeteranHomeowner.com**

You can also get a copy of your local newspaper and look in the real estate section for builders and projects. If you take a look at ads and even read the articles, you can get a good idea of what builders are active in your area. They will probably have a website that you can visit which may provide the types of homes they are building and the prices you can expect to pay.

Questions and Recommendations

Ask questions and seek recommendations from your friends, family and your real estate agent in regards to the homes on your list. This can be a good way to find out the good, bad and the ugly when it comes to selecting a builder. You can also ask the builder to provide you with a list of reviews and references of recent homebuyers.

Do a Drive-By Visit

Here is something that I highly recommend and that is to visit one of the properties. Pick a beautiful Saturday or Sunday morning to drive to one of the new home builder's communities. Hopefully, the homeowners are outside doing some early morning or afternoon chores. This is an opportunity for you to get feedback from the homeowner's mouth. Grab your pen and a pad and then walk around and introduce yourself as a potential new homeowner. As you come upon some of the homeowners, introduce yourself and begin to ask them some questions such as: Are you happy with your new home? Do you have complaints, issues or problems? If so, were they addressed in a timely manner? Do you recommend this builder and would you buy another home from them again?

Hopefully this will give you a good idea of whether or not you can trust this builder to construct the home of your dreams. Last but not least, don't forget to contact the Better Business Bureau for a list of complaints and issues that may have been filed. Also make sure the builder has been approved by the VA.

Preexisting Homes really require Due Diligence

The preexisting or used home requires you to have a keen eye and a knowledge of what's being presented before signing a contract. If you don't have any knowledge of homes, bring someone knowledgeable with you. Think about this the same way you do when you go car shopping, especially used cars. If you know nothing about cars, hopefully you take someone with you who can tell just by taking a test drive if that car has some underlying issues. When it comes to a used home, those underlying issues could cost you thousands of dollars if they are not discovered or disclosed. I want to remind you of this as we covered it in chapter two. The VA does not require a home inspection but it is highly recommended by myself and other industry professionals. Getting a home inspection will give you a good chance to have any big problems exposed before you settle on the home. Also don't be afraid to ask your real estate agent to gather answers to any questions that you may have. That is what he or she is there for.

When you visit the homes that fit your criteria, do a walk around and look at the following items that I have created on this list. I put this list together in order to give an idea of what you may need to address. Rate the items on this list from 1-5. (1 being poor and 5 being excellent). This is just a preliminary list. If there are other items that you wish to rate, you may add them to your notes section.

Your Walk-around Inspection

Siding	_____	Bathrooms	_____
Windows	_____	Flooring	_____
Foundation	_____	Heat and Air Conditioning	_____
Landscaping	_____	Ceiling and Walls	_____
Deck or Patio	_____	Lighting	_____
Fencing	_____		
Kitchen appliances	_____		

*Notes

_____

_____

_____

_____

_____

_____

_____

Lead Paint Awareness

Federal regulations require sellers of pre-1978 residential dwellings to disclose the presence of known lead-based paint in the property. This was enacted to protect you the buyer. The seller of the property has duties of disclosure when it comes to lead paint such as:

- Sellers must disclose known lead-based paint and lead-based paint hazards and provides available reports to buyers and tenants.

- Sellers must give buyers and renters a federal pamphlet titled Protect Your Family From Lead in Your Home.

- Homebuyers will get a 10-day period to conduct a lead-based paint inspection or risk assessment at their own expense if desired. The number of days can be changed by mutual consent.

- Sellers must include certain language in sales contracts and leasing agreements to ensure that disclosure and notification actually take place.

- Sellers, lessors, and real estate professionals share responsibility for ensuring compliance.

Your state may have more guidance and procedures in regard to lead paint poisoning and prevention and/or hazard. Speak with your real estate agent in regard to this subject.

Discovering those wood destroying insects

One of the biggest threats to a home comes in the form of those tiny little wood destroying insects that silently and invisibly consume or live in wood from the sills of your foundation to the rafters of your roof. A nation-wide pest control company named Orkin reports, "Wood-destroying insects cause more than $1 billion a year in property damage in the United States." To discover these little critters it's better to have a professional take care of this. But if you want to include a search in your walk around, you can locate infestation by poking wood with a screwdriver; if the tip goes in easily or you hear a hollow sound when you tap the wood with the handle, you might have a problem.

Be on the lookout for a thin gritty gray-brown film on the surface of damaged material. Also look for narrow mud tubes on both the interior and exterior of the homes walls and foundation. Termites travel though these tubes between their colony below the ground and their dinner above a.k.a. your potential home.

The one time they come out in the open is when they swarm. Swarms consist of flying "reproductives" that leave the colony, mainly in spring, to mate and start new colonies. You may not spot the swarm itself because the love bugs shed their wings and head underground within a few hours.

Instead, look for discarded wings that resemble fish scales. Swarms can emerge indoors or outdoors. Evidence of an indoor swarm, such as discarded wings or the corpses of termites that couldn't find a way out, is a sure sign your home is infested.

I know this was a lot of information for you to digest but don't worry, you will be required to get termite inspection completed as it is part of the process. Just remember, if you don't see them on the surface, that doesn't eliminate the fact that wood destroying insects may exist in the home.

Buying a home is a big financial commitment, so it's crucial to know what you're getting into before you put down your money. An uneducated purchase can result in a lot of time and money lost down the road. To save your cash and heartache, be sure to look closely at any prospective home you are planning to purchase.

HOMEBUYER'S NOTES

"The sellers are willing to give you their organs when they die, Grandma's super-secret recipe for butterscotch brownies, pick of the litter if their dog ever has puppies, a lifetime supply of free zucchini from the garden at their new house, your choice of one free item from their first garage sale..."

Reprinted by permission. Drawing by Randy Glasbergen

CHAPTER 9 – WHAT STAYS AND WHAT GOES

---

*"The light is what guides you home,
the warmth is what keeps you there."*

~ Ellie Rodriguez

When you are previewing a home, it may be easy to remember the big items that stand out, but when you are looking at multiple homes in the same weekend, it all becomes a blur. I can see you asking yourself, "Did that beautiful home on Jones Avenue have a fireplace? Was the basement finished? What about the closet space in the kid's room, did it have enough room for all their clothes? Does that home on Smith Avenue have a public water system or does the water supply come from a well? Is the heating system oil, gas or electric with forced hot air? How about central air?" These are important things to know, right? When you look at a home, you may take some notes but for the most part, you trust your memory. Your memory may work well if you are looking at model homes but guess what? The things you see in a model home are for the model home, and a lot of those things are optional and upgradeable items. This chapter is for the person who buys an existing home. A home that has all the bells and whistles to include drapes to die for. When you are looking at a pre-existing home, you have to take good notes and remember, everything is negotiable.

Does it stay or Does it go...

When looking at an existing home a.k.a. a home that someone currently lives in, you are going to see things that you may want to stay with the house, and things that you don't want to see when you move in. Everything from windows to water softeners to freezers and fireplace screen doors, you have the option to request that it stays or demand that it's removed by your move in date.

Understanding Inclusions

This is where you, as the buyer, are making a statement to the seller saying you intend for certain annotated items to be included in the sale of the property unless otherwise negotiated.

To me, this is the fun part of finding your home, especially when that home has items that you love or need. This is the time when you have to slow down and think about what you need for your new home. Go back into the pre-planning phase and ask yourself questions such as, "If I find a home with a nice washer and dryer, do I ask the owner to leave it behind or should I buy my own?" Remember, we are talking about an existing home not new construction. When buying new construction, you get the appliances that they provide (they come with the house) and in most cases, their selections are pretty good.

Back to the pre-planning phase. What do you want included, or in other words, what would you prefer for Mr. and Mrs.

homeowner to leave behind? In the real estate world, these are called inclusions. Before I start explaining what can go and what can stay, I want to go over something called fixtures. Fixtures are things permanently attached to a home. Here is an example. You really love the wet bar that Mr. Homeowner built down in the finished basement area. You take a good look at it and it's affixed to the wall. Then guess what, it's not going anywhere; you get it with the house. Let's look at the other side of the bar (so to speak). Mr. Homeowner has a nice German crafted wet bar that he had made while stationed at Ramstein AB. You can tell that the craftsmanship is amazing. Even the stools fit perfectly with the design. You fall in love with the wet bar and you want it. Does it stay with the house? It probably should because if you know anything about German furniture, it's pretty heavy! Well, I am not going to give you the answer until the end of this chapter. So let's move on to what I call the Inclusion Memory Jogger. (IMJ)

Let's take a tour through a make-believe home and play a little game of what stays and what goes. We will start in the front of the home and move around.

As we open the door and either on the right side or the left side of the door you see and alarm pad.

Question: Would the alarm system transfer over to me or will the homeowner be taking it with them? If the alarm system is hard wired throughout the house then it comes with the house but we are in the 21st Century and there are a lot of wireless systems on the market. So for the sake of bringing us up to modern times, let's use the wireless option. You make a note in your (IMJ) that you want the alarm system. Now that you are walking through the foyer, you see a beautiful ceiling fan hanging down in the family room. It's amazing and as you watch it turn you notice that it's super quiet. You like it don't you? So how can you make it yours? The first step is to check off — Ceiling Fan(s) in your IMJ. Then when you make your offer, make sure you include this item as something you want when writing the contract.

Let's cover a few more items to make sure you fully understand inclusions.

As you walk toward the kitchen you see a room with a nice washer and dryer in it. You are thinking about how nice it would be to not have to buy a washer and dryer. So you begin to look at your IMJ and see clothes dryer and clothes washer and check them both off. You turn around and walk toward the family room. When you look toward the windows you notice draperies and curtain rods that fit this room perfectly. Again you begin to think, do I want to go shopping for drapes or do I want to ask the homeowner to make it part of the deal? What the heck, it doesn't hurt to ask so again, you check it off on your IMJ. By now I am sure you get an idea when it comes to inclusions. It's basically selecting what you want the seller to leave behind. It may be something you really need or it may be something that you really like. Like I said before, it doesn't hurt to ask! There may be additional things that are not included in the IMJ that you may ask for. One of the items I can think of is a homeowner's warranty program. If you know that a homeowner has a homeowner's warranty program in effect, then ask for the seller to pay for a certain number of years as part of the deal. I didn't forget about that German crafted wet bar. Even though it's heavy and probably very hard to move out of the house, it's not a fixture. So if you want it, you can put it in the contract as an inclusion. You get it? Good!

What about the excluded items

Exclusions are a part of the process as it allows you to annotate what you want removed from the home before you move in. Let's go back to the same scenario of you walking into a beautiful home. As you walk into the foyer you see the drapes hanging from the windows. You make a comment to yourself saying those drapes are so ugly they need to be removed from the premises and burned immediately. You want to make sure that when you move in, they are nowhere to be seen. Sounds like an exclusion right? Okay, let's go around the house and see what else stands out like a sore thumb that is not attached to the home. We are now walking into the living room and what do we see? It looks like a ceiling fan but it's decorated in the colors and logo of the homeowner's favorite football team. Let's say you are a football fan and your favorite team plays in Baltimore and you walk into a home that has a ceiling fan decorated in Pittsburg football black and yellow or gold or whatever their color may be, you are now saying to yourself, *Oh no, that has to go!* It's something about a sports fan when it comes to their favorite teams. People will put things in their house that they like but it may not be your cup of tea. It can be anything that you may want excluded but remember, it can't be a fixture. It must be a removable object. Let's go back to the washing and dryer. You have a nice washer and dryer that you purchased a few months ago and you can't wait to try it out in your new home. If you want to make sure the owner removes theirs, put it on the exclusion list. As you can probably see, the exclusion list carries a similar amount of weight as the inclusion list. I will give you enough room in your IMJ to annotate your exclusions in the remarks section. Remember, don't assume anything, if you want it, tell the seller via the contract. It's all about you when it comes to buying a home. This reminds me of the old saying, "You never know if you don't ask!"

Inclusions Memory Jogger (IMJ) Use this tool to remind you of items in a property that you want included in the contract (Big Screen TVs may need some extra negotiation but I threw it in there anyway!)

If there are items in the property that you want removed, place them in your notes as exclusions.

INCLUDED	INCLUDED	INCLUDED
___Alarm Systems	___Exhaust Fans(s)	___Patio Furniture
___Microwave	___Freezer	___Shades/Blinds
___Ceiling Fan(s)	___Humidifier	___Storage shed
___Clothes Dryer	___Garage Opener(s)	___Oven
	___Hot Tub,	
___Clothes Washer	Equipment & Cover	___Intercom System
	___Pool, Equipment &	___Playground
___Curtains/Rods	Cover	Equipment
___Electronic Air Filter	___Refrigerator	___Pools
___Window AC Units	___Window Fans	___Dishwasher
___Big Screen TV (s)	___Bar and Bars Stools	___Chandeliers
___Water Softener		

Exclusion Notes

_____

_____

_____

_____

_____

_____

_____

_____

_____

_____

_____

_____

_____

_____

_____

_____

HOMEBUYER'S NOTES

"I opened my checkbook. Then I opened it again.
Then I opened it again. Then I opened it again.
So how come the bank called it a 'closing'?"

Reprinted by permission. Drawing by Randy Glasbergen

CHAPTER 10 – THE CLOSING

*"Owning a home is a keystone of wealth —
both financial affluence and emotional security."*

~ Suze Orman

I remember closing on my home as if it were just yesterday. The agent brought me over to the house for a final inspection. It was amazing to smell the newness of this house. The carpet was clean, the walls were fresh and the windows were spotless. At this point, I was really beginning to feel accomplished. This was the day of the walkthrough. As I went through each room in the house, I learned something new in regard to homeownership. The tour included simple items like where my water shut off valve was located, how to find and operate the circuit breakers and where to locate all the manuals for the new appliances. My agent started in the basement and we worked our way thought the entire home. When it comes to the walk through this is the final chance to make sure that everything in regard to the house is right. This is where the butterflies really start to set in. Your big day is here and you will soon receive your keys, but there are a few more steps that have to occur.

The Closing

During the early stage of my home buying process I remember working with a representative from a title company. Their primary responsibilities were to review and research the title to my soon to be property to ensure a transfer free of defects that could prevent the sale. They funded the transaction, recorded the legal documents and guaranteed my transaction by offering title insurance. Title insurance issued to my lender on my behalf was used to protect the lender's interest and the owner's policy was put in place to protect my interest. The title company you select will work closely with your lender and real estate agent throughout the entire process. Although you may have limited interaction until a few days prior to settlement, the Title Company is an essential part of your team! So as you can see, the title company plays a big role in making sure everything goes as smooth as can be. That's the goal anyway, right?

That brings us to settlement or what is more commonly known as the closing. This is the final step in the home buying process. It's where you get to see and understand how all of the pieces come together. The settlement or closing is conducted by a Licensed Settlement/Escrow Officer or in some state a Licensed Attorney.

Thinking back to this important day, I remember saying to myself, "The time has finally arrived, I am about to officially become a home owner." Together with the Settlement/Escrow Officer, Listing Agent, Selling Agent, Sellers and myself, I began to witness the important role each team member played. Each party had to play their part in order for this process to end smoothly. Even though the process was set up for success, something did occur that was a total shock. The Settlement/Escrow Officer gave me a big stack of papers that required my review and signature. Actually, this was expected but I must admit, I honestly had a picture in my head of sitting down, signing a few papers, getting my keys and heading home. As you can probably figure out, I didn't expect a whole book full of papers for me to review and sign. Okay, maybe it was not exactly a book but it was a nice size stack. Each document was important as each one served a different purpose. There were disclosures, disclaimers and agreements for me to acknowledge and sign. I felt like I really needed to focus on each document as I was about to make the biggest purchase of my life. This was really a learning process for sure. I witnessed how at closing, transfer taxes were paid and other items were also settled including closing costs, legal fees, and adjustments. I even remember seeing my agent smiling from ear to ear as he received a nice size commission check. But you know what, my agent earned it as he did a great job. After one last signature, the settlement officer looks over to me, smiled, handed me the door keys to my new home and said, "Congratulations Sergeant Bailey, you are now a home owner!"

Note – Escrow/Closing/Settlement Services are jurisdictional and you should verify the laws within your own state.

All these papers, now what

You just closed on your new home. You have keys in hand and the moving company is on the way to drop off your household goods. Before you walk out the door, someone yells out to you, "Hey, don't forget your paperwork!"

What do you do with all of these papers? Take them to your new home and place them in a safe place! These papers are the proof that you are a homeowner. When I got settled into my new home I went out to an office supply store and purchased a two-drawer filing cabinet. I also purchased some file folders with labels. I knew that I had to be organized, not just with my homeownership paperwork but with all of my important papers. The most important word in this chapter is the word *organized*. Now that you are a homeowner, you have to keep track of all things related to homeownership. My folders gave me a simple way to find what I needed when I needed it. I began labeling the folders as: mortgage documents, mortgage statements, and mortgage insurance.

I also created a folder holder for my car documents which includes statements, repairs and recalls etc. Banking statements, which allowed me to have a record of my expenses by month are also included. And of course, my settlement papers are in their own section which includes all of my documents such as the deed, purchase agreement, plat, etc.

There may be a time when you will need these documents in the future. It's imperative that you know where they are without playing the guessing game at a later date. However you decide to package your settlement documents is totally up to you, but again the key word is organization.

HOMEBUYER'S NOTES

©Glasbergen
glasbergen.com

"Honey, you promised to add a deck
and patio ages ago. *I'm still waiting!*"

Reprinted by permission. Drawing by Randy Glasbergen

THE CONCLUSION

"The great thing in this world is not so much where you stand, as in what direction you are moving."
~ Oliver Wendell Holmes

You Can Do It

Going through the homebuying process will be a different experience for everyone. Let's say you may have perfect credit and a co-worker or a friend wants to sell you their home. You have already selected a great real estate agent and lender based on a recommendation. For you, this process *may* be very easy. If you notice I said may be very easy! I am not going to say it *will* be easy because you never know what will surface during the journey. But if you keep in mind the steps outlined in this book, you will keep your problems to a minimum.

This process is not one that you go at alone. You must enlist a good real estate agent to help you along the way. Even if you are looking at new construction, get a real estate agent to represent you in a buyer's agent agreement. The builder will have a sales representative holding down the fort in the sales office, but who do you think that person represents? Having a real estate agent who represents you will give you more negotiation power.

Speaking of power, when you make up your mind to buy a home, you must be all in. If you have road blocks due to credit, debt to income ratio, or less than perfect financial planning, you must remain strong from beginning to end. You can overcome most credit issues even if it takes you a little longer than you expect it to; it will be worth the wait. If your debt to income ratio is higher than desired, it only means you have to pay down some of your debt and with the VA no money down benefit, you may be in a position to use your cash to eliminate some of that debt. I remember a saying from when I was a little boy and it went like this, "Where there is a will, there is a way!"

Once you get past the initial financial requirements, you will be on house hunting duty. Hopefully, you find the home that fits your requirement in a timely manner. But remember; don't let anyone rush you into a decision. Your selection is not about what the real estate agent likes or even other outside parties, it's all about you and your financial qualifications.

Once you select the home, the VA will go into protecting their asset mode by requiring you to have a VA Home Loan inspection. But that doesn't replace the need for an independent home inspection performed by a home inspection professional. Having a home inspection completed is really a blessing in disguise, as an inspection will help you really determine if this house is right for you. Who wants a house that has a roof that leaks or faulty electrical wiring? Let the experts determine if your house is considered, "All Clear!"

As you prepare for the closing on your new home, don't put anything on your credit. Your lender will tell you this is the death of many homebuying deals. I was recently reading a story of a soon to be homeowner who thought buying a few items on credit would not show up before the closing occurred. They believed the salesman at the furniture store and purchased a living room set and had it set for delivery soon after the projected closing date. Well, I probably don't have to tell you what happened. To make a long story short, the closing never happened as the client's debt to income ratio was outside of the maximum requirement. So close, but yet so far!

As you probably know from reading the testimonials located in the beginning of this book, using the VA home loan program has been such a blessing to many families. It has allowed our veterans to hold on to their savings, move into a house when they couldn't afford to rent an apartment.

Don't let this opportunity pass you by. Being a military veteran affords you many tremendous opportunities. The ability to buy a home using the VA Loan is one of the greatest gifts that you will receive and that you deserve for serving in the best military in the world.

In conclusion, I want to share one more VA Loan "Success Story" with you and this one comes from Chicago, Illinois.

"Brian, where were you 21 years ago when my husband Derrick and I almost gave up on buying our dream home with his veterans benefits? Even though we made numerous calls to The Veterans Administration we couldn't get many of our questions answered. I thank God for not giving up. One day a kind lady at the office of Veterans Affairs could feel our frustration over the phone. She calmed me down, she told me everything was going to be alright and that she was going to make sure of that. First, she helped us acquire his DD214 (his Army discharge papers) which at that time wasn't easy to get either. From getting the DD214 to getting our eligibility certificate to finding a house to closing on our house, she allowed us to call her with any question we had. Not only that, she called and checked up on us as well. She was and still is our Guardian Angel. We know that what she did for us was over and beyond her job description. Countless times over the years as we have raised our kids while enjoying our home I think of her and wonder how she is doing. I also think of the veterans who either don't know about this benefit or have run up against a brick wall trying to get through this process. A book like the one you have written would have been heaven sent. I pray that your book gets into the hands of each and every person that needs it. My name is Kitten Gray. I am the dignified wife of Captain Derrick Gray and I approve this message."

Thank for you purchasing this book and may your homebuying purchase bring you many years of enjoyment! ~ Brian K. Bailey

GLOSSARY OF REAL ESTATE TERMS

Adjustable Rate Mortgage (ARM) These types of mortgages have interest rates that can fluctuate based the economic landscape. Most ARMs allow for an annual rate change based on the one-year Treasury bill index.

Amendments Changes to previous approved and adopted written agreements.

Agreement of Sale A written agreement by which the purchaser agrees to buy certain real estate and the seller agrees to sell, on the terms and conditions set forth in the contract.

Americans with Disabilities Act (ADA) A federal Law effective in 1992, designated to eliminate discrimination against individuals with disabilities.

Annual Percentage Rate (APR) This rate reflects the total cost of borrowing money, including the interest rate and other costs built into the loan amount. The interest rate and the APR are typically different, and veterans should look at both when comparing VA lenders. Two loans can have similar interest rates, but the one with a higher APR will cost more.

Amortization The liquidation of a financial burden by installment payments, which include principle and interest.

Appraisal A professional appraiser's opinion of the property's market value.

Appraised Value An estimate of the property's present worth.

Base Allowance for Housing (BAH) A service member's BAH can be included as monthly income. Housing allowances can help defray or entirely cover monthly mortgage payments.

Balloon Payment The final payment of a mortgage that is considerably larger than the required periodic payments because the loan amount was not fully amortized.

Budget A statement of estimated income and expenses for a period of time. A plan for using money.

Buyer's Agent A real estate agent who represents only the buyer of a property in a real estate transaction. This type of agent agrees to exclusively represent the best interest of the buyer, usually under a formal contract.

Buydown A payment made, often by the seller, to help the buyer qualify for the loan.

Caveat emptor A Latin phrase meaning, "Let the buyer beware."

Certificate of Eligibility This is a formal VA document that delineates what entitlement, if any, a prospective borrower has available. It is the only acceptable method to document entitlement.

Clear to close This means that any loan conditions have been satisfied to the underwriter's satisfaction and the borrower is ready to formally close on the home purchase.

Closing cost These are charges and fees associated with finalizing a loan. The VA limits what veterans can pay in closing costs to a 1 percent lender origination fee, reasonable discount points and other reasonable and standard fees and charges.

Comparable Sales Also known as "comps." These are recently sold properties that are similar in size, location and other key facets to a home being purchased.

Conditional Approval A loan with conditional approval will be issued as long as the veteran meets the requirements and stipulations spelled out by the underwriter.

Contingencies A provision of condition in the purchase of real estate requiring a certain act to be done or an event to happen before the contract becomes binding.

Contract An agreement entered into by two or more legally competent parties by the terms of which one or more of the parties, for a consideration, undertakes to do or to refrain from doing some legal act or acts, or bilateral, where all parties to the instrument are legally bound to act as prescribed.

Conveyance A written instrument that evidences transfer of some interest in real property from one person to another.

Credit Scoring A three digit score that assesses a borrower's credit risk and the probability of default based on his or her past pay performances, outstanding credit balances, time on file, and number or search inquires.

DD-214 This is an official VA document that explains a veteran's discharge information. Reservists and National Guard members, who don't have a single discharge certificate like the DD-214, should procure their latest annual retirement points summary along with evidence of their honorable service

Debt To Income Ratio (DTI) This is the ratio of your total monthly debt payments to your gross monthly income. VA-approved lenders use 41 percent as a benchmark. Your Debt to Income Ratio can change depending on the loan amount you seek.

Deed A written instrument that when executed and delivered conveys title to or an interest in real estate.

Discount Points A point is equal to 1 percent of the loan amount. Borrowers can pay points to buy down their interest rate. Paying points is relatively infrequent among most VA borrowers.

Exclusive Agency A contractual agreement under which the listing broker acts as the **agent** or as the legally recognized non-agency representative of the seller(s), and the seller(s) agrees to pay a commission to the listing broker if the property is sold through the efforts of any **real estate** broker.

Earnest Money Deposit (EMD) Borrowers put this into an escrow account when the time comes to purchase a home. These good faith funds can be put toward closing costs or refunded to the borrower. The amount depends on several factors, including geography and the property.

Entitlement Refers to the amount of money the U.S. Department of Veterans Affairs would be willing to back for qualified VA-eligible borrower. The VA provides this backing to the lender, to encourage lenders to make loans toveterans.

Escrow Account An account where monies are held by a third-party on behalf of transacting parties.

Executory Contract A Contract under which something remains to be done by one of more of the parties.

Expressed Contract An oral or written contract in which the parties state their terms and express their intentions in words.

Fair Credit Reporting Act (FCRA) is the act that regulates the collection of credit information and access to your credit report. It was passed in 1970 to ensure fairness, accuracy and privacy of the personal information contained in the files of the credit reporting agencies.

Fair Housing Act of 1968 The Term for Title VIII of the Civil Rights Act of 1968 as amended, which prohibits discrimination based on race, color, sex, religion, national origin, handicaps, and familial status in the sale of rental and residential property.

Fannie Mae The Federal National Mortgage Association (FNMA), usually known as Fannie Mae, is a government-sponsored enterprise that buys loans from mortgage lenders, packages them together, and sells them as a mortgage-backed security to investors on the open market.

FICO Stands for Fair Issac Corp., a California-based company that created the first-ever credit score. This is the lending industry's preferred credit score. FICO scores run from 300 to 850.

Fixtures A fixture, as a legal concept, means any physical property that is permanently attached (fixed) to real property (usually land) Property not affixed to real property is considered chattel property. Fixtures are treated as a part of real property, particularly in the case of a security interest.

Federal Housing Administration (FHA) A federal administrative body created by the National Housing Act in 1934 to encourage improvement in housing standards and conditions, to provide an adequate home-financing system through the insurance of housing mortgages and credit, and to exert a stabilizing influence on the mortgage market.

Fee Simple Estate The maximum possible estate or right of ownership of real property continuing forever.

FHA Loans A mortgage issued by federally qualified lenders and insured by the Federal Housing Administration (FHA). FHA loans are designed for low-to-moderate income borrowers who are unable to make a large down payment. As of 2017, these loans allow the borrower to borrow up to 96.5% of the value of the home; the 3.5% down payment requirement can come from a gift or a grant, which makes FHA loans popular with first-time homebuyers

Fixed Rate Mortgage Interest rates cannot fluctuate on a fixed-rate mortgage. The most common fixed-rate terms are 15 years and 30 years.

Foreclosure The action of taking possession of a mortgaged property when the mortgagor fails to keep up their mortgage payments.

Freddie Mac (FHLMC) is a stockholder-owned, government-sponsored enterprise (GSE) chartered by Congress in 1970 to keep money flowing to mortgage lenders in support of homeownership and rental housing for middle income Americans.

Funding Fee A set fee applied to every purchase loan or refinance. The proceeds go directly to the VA and help cover losses on the few loans that go into default. Borrowers with service-connected disabilities can secure an exemption from the VA Funding Fee. Regular military members pay slightly lower Funding Fees than Reservists and National Guard members.

Grants Federal grants can be an important source of funding for the first time home buyer. Unlike a loan or mortgage, a grant does not have to be repaid. These programs are usually targeted to areas where the government wants to invest in the revitalization of a community.

Guaranty A promise made by the federal government to lenders that it will repay a portion of the loan should a borrower default. Loans backed by guaranties are generally considered lower risk.

Home Owners Warranty is a service contract that covers essential applications and home system components when they break down due to normal wear and tear.

HUD The Department of Housing and Urban Development.

Interest A charge made by the lender for the use of money.

Interest Rate The rate that determines how much a lender charges a borrower in exchange for lending money. Interest rates are expressed as percentages of the total loan. Interest rates can vary widely depending on market conditions, size of the loan and a borrower's credit score.

Interim Financing A short term loan usually made during the construction phase of a building project, often referred to as a construction loan.

Joint Tenancy The ownership of real estate by two or more parties who have been named in one conveyance as Joint tenants.

Judgement The official and authentic decision of a court on the respective right and claims of the parties to an action or suit.

Legal Description The description of a specific parcel of real estate sufficient for an independent surveyor to locate and identify it.

Loan Processor A person that gathers together all of the outstanding documents and information once a borrower has signed a purchase contact. Their job is to piece together loan applications for an underwriter.

Lien A right given by law to certain creditors to have their debts paid out of the property of a defaulting debtor.

Lock Fee Some lenders charge borrowers for rate locks, depending on the time period, the rate and other factors. As a veteran you should ask lenders about lock fees when you're doing your comparison shopping and interviews.

Listing Agent. A listing agent is a real estate agent that helps homeowners sell their home. Listing agents list client homes on the MLS and negotiate the best possible price and terms for the home seller. While buyer's agents represent home buyers, listing agents represent home sellers. Learn how real estate commission works.

Minimum Property Requirement These are basic health and safety conditions that a property must meet to satisfy the VA. They're also the conditions that make the home sellable. The VA in most cases requires homes to be "move-in ready."

Mortgage A conditional transfer of pledge of real estate as security for the loan. Also the document creating a mortgage lien.

Multiple Listing Service (MLS) Real estate databases and software that allow agents and brokers to look at transactions, home listings and a suite of other information tools. These are private systems unavailable to the general public.

Negative Compensating Factor Compensating factors are strengths on a loan application that can help borrowers secure a loan. Negative compensating factors can do the opposite. Bankruptcies, foreclosures, late payments can all be considered negative compensating factors.

Notice of Value (NOV) This is the VA appraisal, which spells out the independent expert's assessment of the property's value. Ultimately, it's up to a lender's staff appraisal reviewer to issue the final notice of value.

Origination Fee The VA allows lenders to charge borrowers a flat fee of up to 1 percent of the loan amount to cover in-house costs and services.

Permanent Buydown Veterans can pay reasonable discount points to buy down their interest rate. A discount point is 1 percent of the loan amount. Borrowers have to pay this cost up front.

PITI This acronym stands for Principal, Interest, Taxes and Insurance.

PMI Private Mortgage Insurance

Power of Attorney A surrogate with power of attorney can sign contracts and other documents on behalf of an absent service member.

Prequalification This is an unverified, cursory discussion between the lender and the prospective borrower about finances. While prequalification can help you get a sense of what you afford it means little to sellers and real estate agents as they are looking for preapproval letters.

Property Tax A levy on property that the owner is required to pay. The tax is levied by the governing authority of the jurisdiction in which the property is located; it may be paid to a national government, a federated state, a county or geographical region, or a municipality. If you are a 100% disabled veteran you may be exempt from Property Taxes.

Real Estate Agent An individual who is licensed to negotiate and arrange real estate sales; works for a real estate broker. Negotiate and arrange can include showing property, listing property, filling in contracts, listing agreements, and purchase contracts. The Real Estate **broker** has a higher level license than a **real estate** agent and would be authorized to hire **real estate** agents to work under the **broker's** supervision.

Real Estate Broker A higher level license than a real estate agent and would be authorized to hire real estate agents to work under the broker's supervision.

REALTOR® A federally registered collective membership mark which identifies a real estate professional who is member of the NATIONAL ASSOCIATION OF REALTORS® and subscribes to its strict Code of Ethics.

Tenants in Common Share a specified proportion of ownership rights in real property and upon the death of a tenant in common, that share is transferred to the estate of the deceased tenant.

Tenants by entirety A method in some states by which married couples can hold the title to a property. In order for one **spouse** to modify his or her interest in the property in any way, the consent of both spouses is required by tenants by entirety.

Title Insurance Protects the owner of property and the mortgage lender against future claims for any unknown defects in the title to the property at the time of sale.

USDA Loan The United States Department of Agriculture (USDA) offers a loan program for rural borrowers who meet certain income requirements. The program is managed by the Rural Housing Service (RHS), which is part of the Department of Agriculture. This type of mortgage loan is offered to "rural residents who have a steady, low or modest income, and yet are unable to obtain adequate housing through conventional financing." Income must be no higher than 115% of the adjusted area median income [AMI]. The AMI varies by county.

VA Home Loan Started in 1944 through the GI Bill of Rights. The VA home loan was created for veterans to acquire a federally guaranteed loan without a down payment.

Special Bonus

The
Veteran's
Home Buying Journal

THE VETERAN'S HOMEBUYING JOURNAL

This handy journal is essential in keeping you organized while you are searching for that perfect home. I have included a section for you to record some of the important people involved in your transaction such as your real estate agent, lender, title company, home inspector and a section for other resources you may encounter along the way. It also includes a section called "Home Search" as this portion of your journal gives you room to annotate important information about the home to include the property address, type of home, total number of bedrooms and bathrooms, likes, dislikes and added remarks along with room for additional notes. I only made room for 10 properties inside the book but if you want a larger size PDF copy of this journal, register your contact info on **Bonus.TheVeteranHomeowner.com** and I will send you the PDF version personalized with your name on it.

YOUR SUCCESS TEAM

Your Real Estate Agent:_____

Phone#:_____ **Email Address:**_____

Website _____

Your Lender:_____

Phone#:_____ **Email Address:**_____

Website _____

Your Title Company: _____

Phone#:_____ **Email Address:**_____

Website _____

Your Home Inspector: _____

Phone#:_____ **Email Address:**_____

Website _____

Other Resources: _____

_____

_____

HOME SEARCH NOTES

YOUR HOME SEARCH

Property Address and Location:

_____

_____

Type of home (Townhome or Single Family)

_____

Bedrooms / Bathrooms

_____ _____

Likes:

_____

_____

_____

_____

_____

_____

_____

Dislikes:

_____

_____

_____

_____

_____

Remarks:

_____

_____

_____

_____

_____

_____

_____

HOME SEARCH NOTES

YOUR HOME SEARCH

Property Address and Location:

_____

_____

Type of home (Townhome or Single Family)

_____

Bedrooms / Bathrooms

_____ _____

Likes:

_____

_____

_____

_____

_____

_____

_____

Dislikes:

_____

_____

_____

_____

_____

_____

Remarks:

_____

_____

_____

_____

_____

_____

HOME SEARCH NOTES

YOUR HOME SEARCH

Property Address and Location:

_____

_____

Type of home (Townhome or Single Family)

_____

Bedrooms / Bathrooms

_____ _____

Likes:

_____

_____

_____

_____

_____

_____

_____

_____

Dislikes:

_____

_____

_____

_____

_____

_____

Remarks:

_____

_____

_____

_____

_____

_____

_____

HOME SEARCH NOTES

YOUR HOME SEARCH

Property Address and Location:

_____

_____

Type of home (Townhome or Single Family)

_____

Bedrooms / Bathrooms

_____ _____

Likes:

_____

_____

_____

_____

_____

_____

_____

Dislikes:

_____

_____

_____

_____

_____

_____

Remarks:

_____

_____

_____

_____

_____

_____

HOME SEARCH NOTES

YOUR HOME SEARCH

Property Address and Location:

_____

_____

Type of home (Townhome or Single Family)

_____

Bedrooms / Bathrooms

_____ _____

Likes:

_____

_____

_____

_____

_____

_____

_____

Dislikes:

_____

_____

_____

_____

_____

_____

_____

Remarks:

_____

_____

_____

_____

_____

_____

_____

_____

_____

HOME SEARCH NOTES

YOUR HOME SEARCH

Property Address and Location:

_____

_____

Type of home (Townhome or Single Family)

_____

Bedrooms / Bathrooms

_____ _____

Likes:

_____

_____

_____

_____

_____

_____

_____

Dislikes:

_____

_____

_____

_____

_____

_____

Remarks:

_____

_____

_____

_____

_____

_____

_____

_____

HOME SEARCH NOTES

YOUR HOME SEARCH

Property Address and Location:

_____

_____

Type of home (Townhome or Single Family)

_____

Bedrooms / Bathrooms

_____ _____

Likes:

_____

_____

_____

_____

_____

_____

_____

Dislikes:

_____

_____

_____

_____

_____

_____

Remarks:

_____

_____

_____

_____

_____

_____

_____

ABOUT THE AUTHOR

Brian K. Bailey knew he wanted to join the military at the age of 11. After visiting his Aunt Sandra Jackson who lived near Offutt Air Force Base in Nebraska, he became obsessed with the military way of life. From reading books on Air Power to listening to HF radio frequencies on his transistor radios, Brian knew being around airplanes was his course in life. While still in High School, Brian signed up with the Air Force under the delayed enlistment program in 1983. After graduation in 1984 from Woodlawn Senior High School in Baltimore, Maryland, Brian was Texas bound and headed to the home of Air Force Basic Military Training, Lackland AFB, Texas.

After serving four years in the active component of the U.S. Air Force, Brian transferred to the Maryland Air National Guard serving in the 175th Wing. Five years later, Brian returned to active duty status where he was assigned to the Air National Guard Readiness Center located at Andrews AFB, MD.

Brian retired from military service in 2008 as a Senior Master Sergeant with a career full of wonderful accomplishments and pride. As he transitioned to civilian life, he adopted the Air Force creed as his own motto, *"Integrity first, service before self, and excellence in all we do."*

After his military career, Brian wanted to do something to give back to the organization that did so much for him. He decided to be that much needed advocate for military veterans who want to become a homeowner.

Brian K. Bailey is currently a REALTOR® licensed in the State of Maryland, a Military Relocation Professional (MRP), a member of the Veterans Association of Real Estate Professionals (VAREP), and a Veteran Homeowner.